ENGLISH
FOR EVERYONE

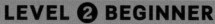

COURSE BOOK
LEVEL ❷ BEGINNER

FREE AUDIO
website and app
www.dkefe.com

Author

Rachel Harding has a background in English-language teaching and is now a full-time author of English-language learning materials. She has written for major English-language publishers including Oxford University Press.

Course consultant

Tim Bowen has taught English and trained teachers in more than 30 countries worldwide. He is the co-author of works on pronunciation teaching and language-teaching methodology, and author of numerous books for English-language teachers. He is currently a freelance materials writer, editor, and translator. He is a member of the Chartered Institute of Linguists.

Language consultant

Professor Susan Barduhn is an experienced English-language teacher, teacher trainer, and author, who has contributed to numerous publications. In addition to directing English-language courses in at least four different continents, she has been President of the International Association of Teachers of English as a Foreign Language, and an adviser to the British Council and the US State Department. She is currently a Professor at the School of International Training in Vermont, USA.

ENGLISH
FOR EVERYONE

COURSE BOOK
LEVEL ❷ BEGINNER

DK

US Editors Allison Singer, Jenny Siklos
Editors Gareth Clark, Lisa Gillespie, Andrew Kerr-Jarrett
Art Editors Chrissy Barnard, Ray Bryant
Senior Art Editor Sharon Spencer
Editorial Assistants Jessica Cawthra, Sarah Edwards
Illustrators Edwood Burn, Denise Joos, Michael Parkin, Jemma
Westing
Audio Producer Liz Hammond
Managing Editor Daniel Mills
Managing Art Editor Anna Hall
Project Manager Christine Stroyan
Jacket Designer Natalie Godwin
Jacket Editor Claire Gell
Jacket Design Development Manager Sophia MTT
Producer, Pre-Production Luca Frassinetti
Producer Mary Slater
Publisher Andrew Macintyre
Art Director Karen Self
Publishing Director Jonathan Metcalf

DK India
Jacket Designer Surabhi Wadhwa
Managing Jackets Editor Saloni Singh
Senior DTP Designer Harish Aggarwal

First American Edition, 2016
Published in the United States by DK Publishing
345 Hudson Street, New York, New York 10014

A catalog record for this book
is available from the Library of Congress.
ISBN 978-1-4654-5185-9

DK books are available at special discounts when purchased
in bulk for sales promotions, premiums, fund-raising, or
educational use. For details, contact: DK Publishing Special
Markets, 345 Hudson Street, New York, New York 10014
SpecialSales@dk.com

Printed and bound in China

All images © Dorling Kindersley Limited
For further information see: www.dkimages.com

A WORLD OF IDEAS:
SEE ALL THERE IS TO KNOW

www.dk.com

Contents

How the course works

English for Everyone is designed for people who want to teach themselves the English language. Like all language courses, it covers the core skills: grammar, vocabulary, pronunciation, listening, speaking, reading, and writing. Unlike in other courses, the skills are taught and practiced as visually as possible, using images and graphics to help you understand and remember. The best way to learn is to work through the book in order, making full use of the audio available on the website and app. Turn to the practice book at the end of each unit to reinforce your learning with additional exercises.

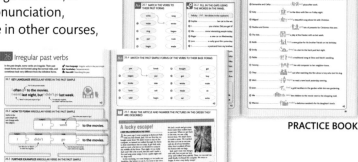

PRACTICE BOOK

COURSE BOOK

Unit number The book is divided into units. The unit number helps you keep track of your progress.

Learning points Every unit begins with a summary of the key learning points.

Modules Each unit is broken down into modules, which should be done in order. You can take a break from learning after completing any module.

Language learning Modules with colored backgrounds teach new vocabulary and grammar. Study these carefully before moving on to the exercises.

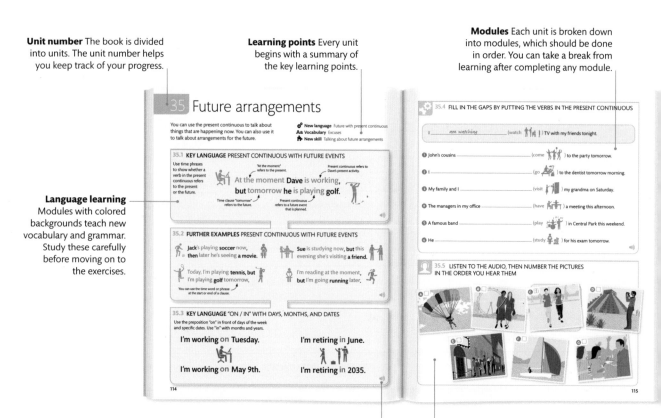

Audio support Most modules have supporting audio recordings of native English speakers to help you improve your speaking and listening skills.

Exercises Modules with white backgrounds contain exercises that help you practice your new skills to reinforce learning.

Language modules

New language points are taught in carefully graded stages, starting with a simple explanation of when they are used, then offering further examples of common usage, and a detailed breakdown of how key constructions are formed.

Module number Every module is identified with a unique number, so you can track your progress and easily locate any related audio.

Module heading The teaching topic appears here, along with a brief introduction.

45.1 KEY LANGUAGE THE PRESENT PERFECT

Use the present perfect to describe something that has happened in the past and which has a result in the present moment.

TIP
Form regular past participles in the same way that you form the past simple, by adding "ed" to the base form of the verb.

"Just" means that the action has happened recently.

Tom has just cleaned the windows.

"Have" or "has" go after the subject in the prefesent perfect.

The main verb goes in its past participle form.

Sample language New language points are introduced in context. Colored highlights make new constructions easy to spot, and annotations explain them.

45.2 FURTHER EXAMPLES THE PRESENT PERFECT

Look! I've just cooked **dinner.**

You haven't cleared **the table. It's a mess!**

John has just washed **the dishes.**

Have you cleaned up **your bedroom?**

Graphic guide Clear, simple visuals help to explain the meaning of new language forms and when to use them, and also act as an aid to learning and recall.

Supporting audio This symbol indicates that the model sentences featured in the module are available as audio recordings.

45.3 HOW TO FORM THE PRESENT PERFECT

SUBJECT + "HAVE" / "HAS"	"JUST"	PAST PARTICIPLE	OBJECT
I have	just	cleaned	the windows.

To make the present perfect, use "have" or "has" with the past participle of the verb.

Formation guide Visual guides break down English grammar into its simplest parts, showing you how to recreate even complex formations.

Vocabulary Throughout the book, vocabulary modules list the most common and useful English words and phrases, with visual cues to help you remember them.

Write-on lines You are encouraged to write your own translations of English words to create your own reference pages.

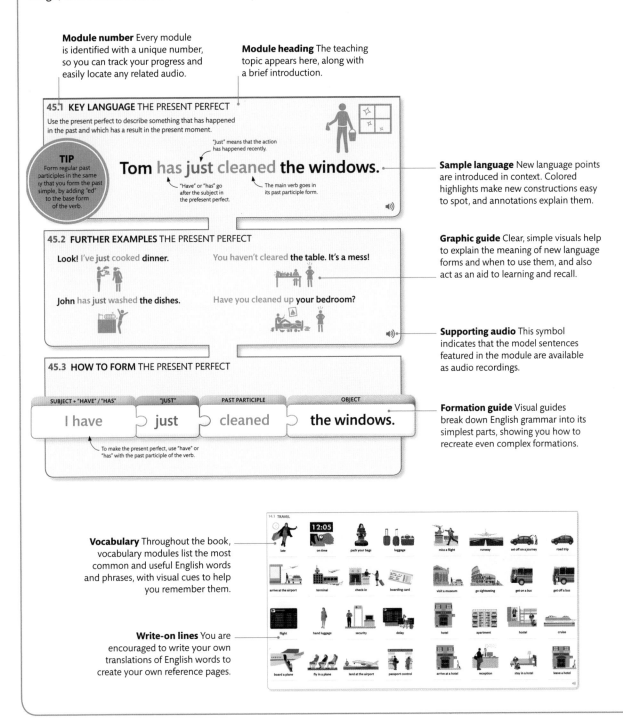

9

Practice modules

Each exercise is carefully graded to drill and test the language taught in the corresponding course book units. Working through the exercises alongside the course book will help you remember what you have learned and become more fluent. Every exercise is introduced with a symbol to indicate which skill is being practiced.

GRAMMAR
Apply new language rules in different contexts.

READING
Examine target language in real-life English contexts.

LISTENING
Test your understanding of spoken English.

VOCABULARY
Cement your understanding of key vocabulary.

WRITING
Practice producing written passages of English text.

SPEAKING
Compare your spoken English to model audio recordings.

Module number Every module is identified with a unique number, so you can easily locate answers and related audio.

Exercise instruction Every exercise is introduced with a brief instruction, telling you what you need to do.

Sample answer The first question of each exercise is answered for you, to help make the task easy to understand.

Space for writing You are encouraged to write your answers in the book for future reference.

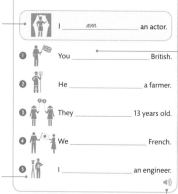

1.5 FILL IN THE GAPS WITH "AM," "IS," OR "ARE"

I ___am___ an actor.

① You _____ British.

② He _____ a farmer.

③ They _____ 13 years old.

④ We _____ French.

⑤ I _____ an engineer.

Supporting graphics Visual cues are given to help you understand the exercises.

Supporting audio This symbol shows that the answers to the exercise are available as audio tracks. Listen to them after completing the exercise.

Speaking exercise This symbol indicates that you should say your answers out loud, then compare them to model recordings included in your audio files.

16.12 SAY THE SENTENCES OUT LOUD, FILLING IN THE GAPS USING SUPERLATIVES

Mount Everest is a very high mountain. It is ___the highest___ mountain in the world.

① Istanbul is a very large city. It is _____ city in Europe.

② The Missouri River is 2,540 miles long. It is _____ river in North America.

③ The cheetah is a very fast animal. It is _____ land animal on Earth.

④ The Kali Gandaki Gorge is 3.46 miles deep. It is _____ gorge in the world.

Listening exercise This symbol indicates that you should listen to an audio track in order to answer the questions in the exercise.

29.4 LISTEN TO THE AUDIO, THEN NUMBER THE PICTURES IN THE ORDER THEY ARE DESCRIBED

Bea talks about her vacation in India.

Audio

English for Everyone features extensive supporting audio materials. You are encouraged to use them as much as you can, to improve your understanding of spoken English, and to make your own accent and pronunciation more natural. Each file can be played, paused, and repeated as often as you like, until you are confident you understand what has been said.

LISTENING EXERCISES
This symbol indicates that you should listen to an audio track in order to answer the questions in the exercise.

SUPPORTING AUDIO
This symbol indicates that extra audio material is available for you to listen to after completing the module.

FREE AUDIO
website and app
www.dkefe.com

Track your progress

The course is designed to make it easy to monitor your progress, with regular summary and review modules. Answers are provided for every exercise, so you can see how well you have understood each teaching point.

Checklists Every unit ends with a checklist, where you can check off the new skills you have learned.

13 ✓ CHECKLIST
🌤 Weather descriptions ☐   **Aa** Temperature words ☐   👤 Talking about the weather ☐

Review modules At the end of a group of units, you will find a more detailed review module, summarizing the language you have learned.

Check boxes Use these boxes to mark the skills you feel comfortable with. Go back and review anything you feel you need to practice further.

NEW LANGUAGE	SAMPLE SENTENCE	☑	UNIT
SAYING YOU'RE NOT FEELING WELL	Are you okay? No, I'm not feeling very well.	☐	11.1
HEALTH PROBLEMS	I have a broken foot. My foot hurts. I have a pain in my head. I have a headache.	☐	11.3, 11.4
TALKING ABOUT THE WEATHER	What's the weather like? Okay, but there are a lot of clouds. It's cloudy.	☐	13.1, 13.2
GIVING THE TEMPERATURE	It's 27 degrees celsius. It's 10 degrees fahrenheit.	☐	13.5
TEMPERATURE PHRASES	How hot is it? It's boiling. How cold is it. It's freezing.	☐	13.5

♻ REVIEW THE ENGLISH YOU HAVE LEARNED IN UNITS 11-13

51

01

1.4 ◀))
① You **are** 40 years old.
② I **am** from New Zealand.
③ He **is** my cousin.
④ We **are** British.
⑤ They **are** mechanics.
⑥ She **is** my sister.
⑦ We **are** scientists.
⑧ She **is** 21 years old.

1.5 ◀))
① You **are** British.
② He **is** a farmer.
③ They **are** 13 years old.
④ We **are** French.
⑤ I **am** an engineer.

1.6 ◀
① True
② False
③ False
④ True
⑤ True

1.7 ◀)) ◀
1. I am Jack.
2. I am 40 years old.
3. I am Canadian.
4. I am an engineer.
5. He is Jack.
6. He is 40 years old.
7. He is Canadian.
8. He is an engineer.
9. They are 40 years old.
10. They are Canadian.

Answers Find the answers to every exercise printed at the back of the book.

Exercise numbers Match these numbers to the unique identifier at the top-left corner of each exercise.

Audio This symbol indicates that the answers can also be listened to.

Talking about yourself

When you want to tell someone about yourself, or about people and things that relate to you, use the present simple form of "to be."

⚙ **New language** Using "to be"
Aa Vocabulary Names, jobs, and family
🧩 **New skill** Talking about yourself

1.1 KEY LANGUAGE "TO BE" STATEMENTS

Use the verb "to be" to talk about your name, age, nationality, and job.

Hi! I am **Noah.** I'm **25 years old.** I'm **Australian** and I'm **a doctor.**

In conversational English, speakers often use contractions. These are shortened versions of pairs of words. "I am" can be shortened to "I'm."

1.2 FURTHER EXAMPLES "TO BE" STATEMENTS

Mia is **72 years old.**

Aban is **a police officer.**

Jack's aunt is **Canadian.**

They are **the Jackson family.**

1.3 HOW TO FORM "TO BE" STATEMENTS

"You" in English is the same in the singular and plural.

These are pronouns. They are the subjects of these sentences.

SUBJECT	"TO BE"	REST OF SENTENCE
I	am	
You	are	
He / She / It	is	**Australian.**
We / They	are	

The verb changes with the subject.

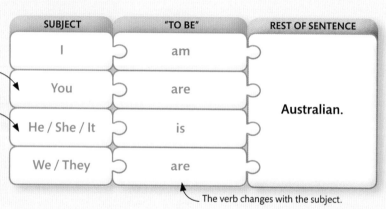

1.12 KEY LANGUAGE "TO BE" QUESTIONS

To ask a "to be" question, put the verb before the subject.

In a statement, the subject comes before the verb.

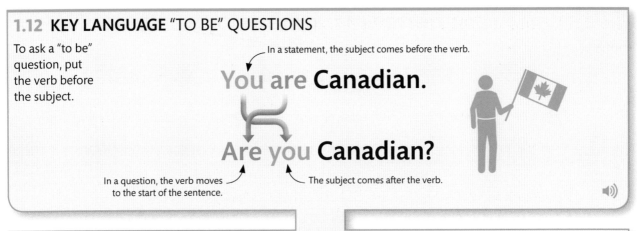

You are **Canadian.**

Are you **Canadian?**

In a question, the verb moves to the start of the sentence.

The subject comes after the verb.

1.13 FURTHER EXAMPLES "TO BE" QUESTIONS

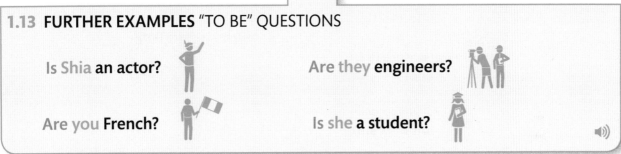

Is Shia **an actor?**

Are they **engineers?**

Are you **French?**

Is she **a student?**

1.14 REWRITE THE SENTENCES AS QUESTIONS

She is a gardener.
Is she a gardener?

1 Alvera is a nurse.
_____

2 Those are my keys.
_____

3 Ruby and Farid are artists.
_____

4 They are best friends.
_____

1.15 SAY THESE QUESTIONS OUT LOUD, FILLING IN THE GAPS

_____*Is*_____ she a waitress?

1 _____ Holly your mother?

2 _____ they from Argentina?

3 _____ these your dogs?

4 _____ this Main Street?

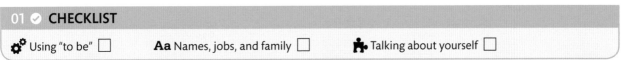

Talking about routines

You can use present simple statements to describe your daily routines, pastimes, and possessions. Use "do" to form negatives and ask questions.

⚙ **New language** The present simple
Aa Vocabulary Routines and pastimes
🧩 **New skill** Talking about routines

2.1 KEY LANGUAGE THE PRESENT SIMPLE

To make the present simple, use the base form of the verb (the infinitive without "to").

This is the base form of the verb "to eat."

I eat lunch at 12 o'clock every day.

She eats lunch at 1:30pm every day.

With "he," "she," and "it," add "s" to the base form.

2.2 FURTHER EXAMPLES THE PRESENT SIMPLE

They go to the gym at 8am.

Jamal goes to the gym at 9am.

Verbs ending "sh," "ch," "o," "ss," "x," and "z" take "es" in the third person singular.

I have a microwave.

She has a dog and a cat.

The verb "have" is irregular. Use "has" for "he," "she," and "it."

2.3 HOW TO FORM THE PRESENT SIMPLE

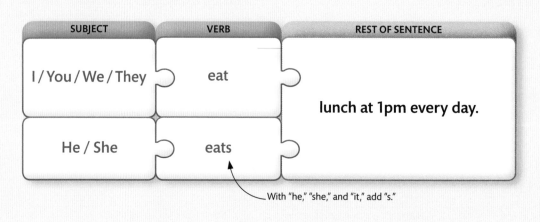

SUBJECT	VERB	REST OF SENTENCE
I / You / We / They	eat	lunch at 1pm every day.
He / She	eats	

With "he," "she," and "it," add "s."

2.4 CROSS OUT THE INCORRECT WORD IN EACH SENTENCE

She ~~eat~~ / eats dinner in the evening.

1. He wake up / wakes up at 7 o'clock.

2. I start / starts work at 10am.

3. They leave / leaves home at 8:45am.

4. We finish / finishes work at 4pm.

5. My friend has / have dinner at 6:30pm.

6. I cook / cooks dinner every night.

7. My parents eat / eats lunch at 2pm.

8. Mia get / gets up at 5 o'clock.

9. My cousin work / works with animals.

2.5 FILL IN THE GAPS USING THE WORDS IN THE PANEL

 Michael ___gets up___ at 7:30am.

1. We _____ work at 5:30pm.

2. Pam _____ lunch at 1:30pm.

3. We _____ in the park.

4. His son _____ work at 9am.

5. My brother _____ work at 4:45pm.

6. They _____ dinner at 8pm.

~~gets up~~   walk   goes to

leaves   eat   eats   leave

2.6 SAY THE SENTENCES OUT LOUD, FILLING IN THE GAPS

Sonia ___goes___ (go) to work early.

1. My son _____ (watch) TV all night.

2. He _____ (go) shopping on Fridays.

3. We _____ (eat) breakfast at 7am.

4. My cousin _____ (work) inside.

5. Georgia _____ (start) work at 9am.

6. They _____ (do) their chores.

2.7 KEY LANGUAGE THE PRESENT SIMPLE NEGATIVE

Use "do not" before the main verb to make the negative. If the subject is "he," "she," or "it," use "does not."

The main verb does not change.

I do not work outside.
I work inside.

He does not work inside.
He works outside.

2.8 FURTHER EXAMPLES THE PRESENT SIMPLE NEGATIVE

You can contract "do not" to "don't" and "does not" to "doesn't."

He does not live in France.

This house doesn't have a yard.

2.9 HOW TO FORM THE PRESENT SIMPLE NEGATIVE

SUBJECT	"DO / DOES" + NOT	VERB BASE FORM	REST OF SENTENCE
I / You / We / They	do not	work	outside.
He / She / It	does not		

2.10 FILL IN THE GAPS TO WRITE EACH SENTENCE THREE DIFFERENT WAYS

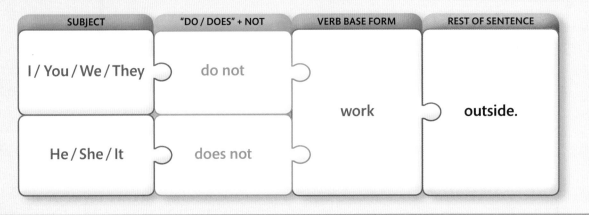

He gets up at 5am.	*He does not get up at 5am.*	*He doesn't get up at 5am.*
1 _____	_____	I don't go to work every day.
2 _____	He does not watch TV in the evening.	_____
3 They work in an office.	_____	_____

2.11 KEY LANGUAGE QUESTIONS WITH "DO" AND "DOES"

For most verbs other than "to be," add "do" or "does" to turn a statement into a question.

You work in an office.

⬇

Do you work in an office?

Use "do" in questions for "I," "you," "we," and "they."

She works in a school.

⬇

Does she work in a school?

Use "does" in questions for "he," "she," and "it."

The main verb is in its base form.

2.12 FURTHER EXAMPLES QUESTIONS WITH "DO" AND "DOES"

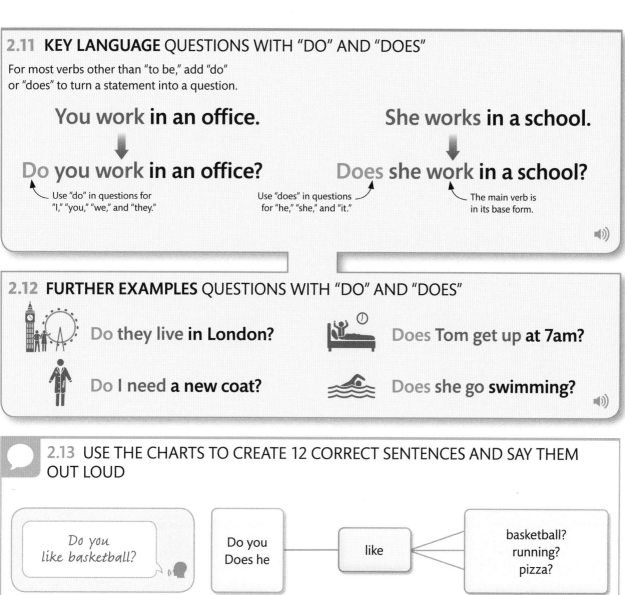

Do they live in London?

Do I need a new coat?

Does Tom get up at 7am?

Does she go swimming?

2.13 USE THE CHARTS TO CREATE 12 CORRECT SENTENCES AND SAY THEM OUT LOUD

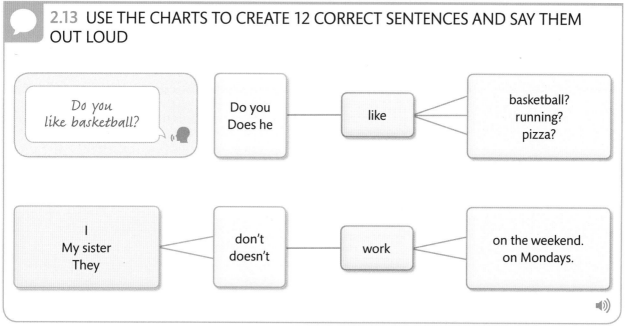

Do you like basketball?

| Do you / Does he | like | basketball? / running? / pizza? |

| I / My sister / They | don't / doesn't | work | on the weekend. / on Mondays. |

03 Today I'm wearing...

You can use the present continuous to describe something that is happening now. It is often used to describe what people are wearing, using, or doing.

⚙️ **New language** The present continuous
Aa Vocabulary Clothes and activities
🧩 **New skill** Talking about what's happening now

3.1 KEY LANGUAGE THE PRESENT CONTINUOUS

Use the present continuous form to describe what is happening right now.

This is the present simple. It describes a regular action.

Julie doesn't usually wear dresses, but today she is wearing a bright red dress.

This is the present continuous. It describes what is happening right now.

3.2 HOW TO FORM THE PRESENT CONTINUOUS

Use "to be" plus the present participle (this is the "-ing" form of the verb) to form the present continuous.

SUBJECT	"TO BE"	VERB + "-ING"	REST OF SENTENCE
She	is	wearing	a red dress.

This is the present participle. These follow the same spelling rules as gerunds.

3.3 FURTHER EXAMPLES THE PRESENT CONTINUOUS

Remember, you can use contractions.

 She is walking **the dog.**

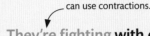 They're fighting **with each other.**

 He is washing **the dishes.**

She is relaxing **at the moment.**

 We are using **our phones.**

For verbs ending in "e" (such as "use"), take off the "e" and add "ing."

 I am cutting **some apples.**

For single-syllable words ending consonant-vowel-consonant, double the final letter before adding "ing."

3.4 CROSS OUT THE INCORRECT WORDS IN THE SENTENCES

> They ~~is~~ / are wearing hats.

1. Sharon is / are reading a book.

2. I am / is carrying my laptop.

3. My cat is / are climbing a tree.

4. We is / are working at the moment.

5. They is / are having their dinner.

6. He is / are talking to his dad.

7. I am / are driving to work right now.

8. They am / are watching the movie.

🔊

3.5 FILL IN THE GAPS TO COMPLETE THE SENTENCES

> She ___is sleeping___ (sleep) in her bed.

1. They _____ (come) home now.

2. We _____ (play) a board game.

3. Jane _____ (cook) dinner.

4. He _____ (drink) some water.

5. We _____ (listen) to music.

6. I _____ (wash) my hair.

7. You _____ (win) the game.

8. We _____ (visit) New Zealand.

🔊

3.6 LISTEN TO THE AUDIO AND MATCH THE PORTRAITS TO THE NAMES

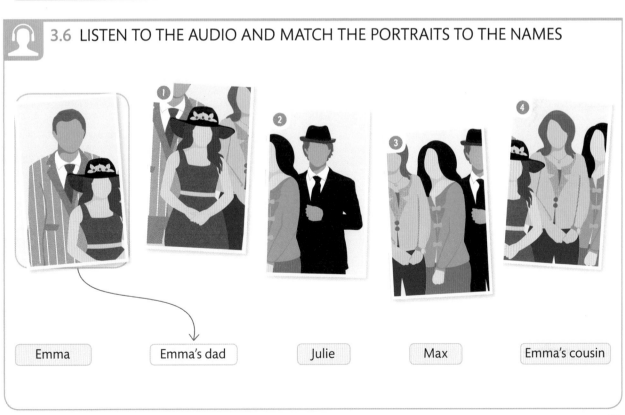

| Emma | Emma's dad | Julie | Max | Emma's cousin |

21

3.7 KEY LANGUAGE THE PRESENT CONTINUOUS NEGATIVE

Make the negative of the present continuous by adding "not" after "to be." Don't change the present participle.

He is wearing **a tie, but** he { is not / isn't } wearing **a hat.**

Add "not" after "to be" to make the negative. You can use contractions, too.

You still use the present participle when you make the negative.

3.8 HOW TO FORM THE PRESENT CONTINUOUS NEGATIVE

SUBJECT	NEGATIVE + "TO BE"	VERB + "-ING"	REST OF SENTENCE
He	isn't	wearing	a hat.

Use the present participle.

3.9 FURTHER EXAMPLES THE PRESENT CONTINUOUS NEGATIVE

 She isn't walking **the dog.**

 We aren't taking **the bus today.**

 They aren't singing **well today.**

 You aren't doing **your job!**

3.10 CROSS OUT THE INCORRECT WORDS IN THE SENTENCES

They ~~isn't~~ / aren't wearing coats.

1. We isn't / aren't playing with them.

2. The baby isn't / aren't sleeping.

3. He isn't / aren't watching the game.

4. You isn't / aren't wearing boots.

5. She isn't / aren't cooking lunch.

6. We isn't / aren't meeting right now.

7. I am not / aren't eating with them.

3.11 FILL IN THE GAPS WITH THE PRESENT CONTINUOUS NEGATIVE

Sheila _isn't walking_ (walk) the dog.

1 They _____ (go) to the park.

2 I _____ (eat) this meal.

3 You _____ (wear) this coat again.

4 Frank's dog _____ (sit) by the fire.

5 My dad _____ (carry) the heavy box.

🔊

3.12 LISTEN TO THE AUDIO AND MARK THE CORRECT ACTIVITIES

Ed's watching TV. ☐
Ed's reading. ☑

1 Dan is sleeping. ☐
   Dan's watching a movie. ☐

2 Manu is dancing. ☐
   Manu's exercising. ☐

3 George's playing his guitar. ☐
   George is singing. ☐

4 Jamal is walking the dog. ☐
   Jamal is playing a computer game. ☐

3.13 SAY POSITIVE AND NEGATIVE SENTENCES BASED ON THE IMAGES

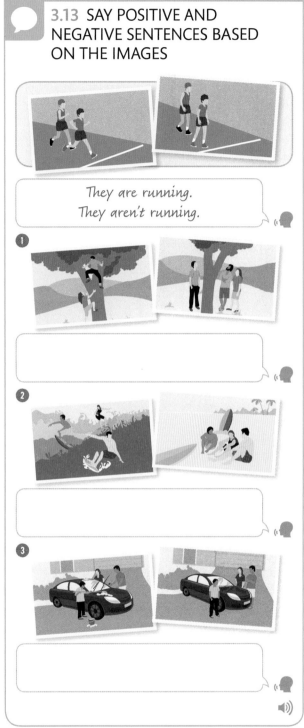

They are running.
They aren't running.

1

2

3

🔊

04 What's happening?

You can use the present continuous to ask about things that are happening now, at the time of speaking.

⚙ **New language** Present continuous questions
Aa Vocabulary Activities and gadgets
🧩 **New skill** Asking about the present

4.1 KEY LANGUAGE PRESENT CONTINUOUS QUESTIONS

Use present continuous questions to ask about what is happening now.

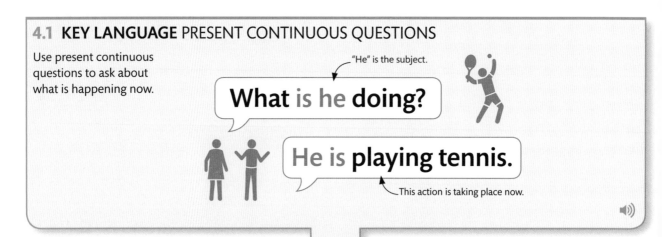

"He" is the subject.

What is he doing?

He is playing tennis.

This action is taking place now.

4.2 HOW TO FORM PRESENT CONTINUOUS QUESTIONS

To make a question in the present continuous, swap the subject and "to be." You can also add question words.

QUESTION WORD	"TO BE"	SUBJECT	VERB + "-ING"
What	**is**	**he**	**doing?**

4.3 FURTHER EXAMPLES PRESENT CONTINUOUS QUESTIONS

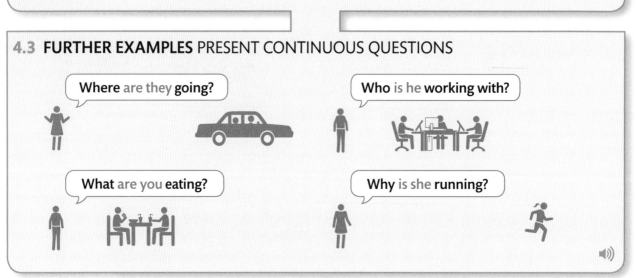

Where are they going?

Who is he working with?

What are you eating?

Why is she running?

4.4 **VOCABULARY** COMMON PRESENT CONTINUOUS VERBS

hold

carry

clean

use

4.5 LISTEN TO THE AUDIO AND WRITE WHO'S DOING EACH ACTIVITY

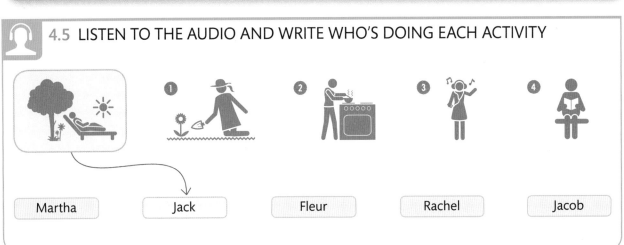

Martha

Jack

Fleur

Rachel

Jacob

Aa 4.6 MATCH THE QUESTIONS TO THE ANSWERS

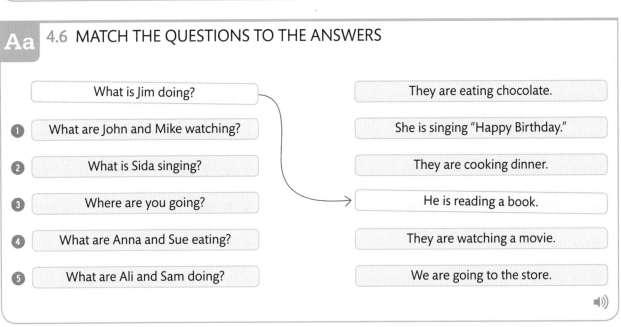

What is Jim doing?

They are eating chocolate.

① What are John and Mike watching?

She is singing "Happy Birthday."

② What is Sida singing?

They are cooking dinner.

③ Where are you going?

He is reading a book.

④ What are Anna and Sue eating?

They are watching a movie.

⑤ What are Ali and Sam doing?

We are going to the store.

4.7 VOCABULARY DIGITAL GADGETS

tablet   computer   smartphone   games console   headphones   e-reader

4.8 FILL IN THE GAPS USING THE PRESENT CONTINUOUS

Jack is _____holding_____ his tablet.

1. Sam is _____ red pants.

2. Jack _____ on an e-reader.

3. You are _____ to headphones.

4. Sam is _____ her bike.

5. I am _____ my smartphone.

reading	cleaning	using
listening	~~holding~~	wearing

4.9 LISTEN TO THE AUDIO, ANSWER THE QUESTIONS

What is Jim holding?
an e-reader ☐   a smartphone ✓

1. What is Lucas cleaning?
his shirt ☐   his shoes ☐

2. What is Orla using?
a computer ☐   a games console ☐

3. What is Livia wearing?
a skirt ☐   a dress ☐

4. What is David doing right now?
writing ☐   reading ☐

5. What is Dewain listening to?
some music ☐   the radio ☐

6. What is Rochelle carrying?
her tablet ☐   her laptop ☐

7. What is Julio using?
his tablet ☐   his e-reader ☐

26

4.10 REWRITE THE QUESTIONS, CORRECTING THE ERRORS

Where Lill is going?
Where is Lill going?

❶ What cleaning is Kimi?

_____

❷ What is doing Jill?

_____

❸ Using what is Jack?

_____

❹ Max what is holding?

_____

❺ Is what carrying Marge?

_____

🔊

4.11 LOOK AT THE PICTURES AND ANSWER THE QUESTIONS, SPEAKING OUT LOUD

What is Alvita wearing?

Alvita is wearing a green sweater.

What are they holding?

Where is Emir going?

What is she carrying?

🔊

05 Types of verbs

You can use most verbs in the continuous form to describe ongoing actions. Some verbs cannot be used in this way. These are called "state" verbs.

⚙ **New language** Action and state verbs
Aa Vocabulary Activities
🧩 **New skill** Using state verbs

5.1 KEY LANGUAGE ACTION AND STATE VERBS

Action verbs usually describe what people or things do. State verbs usually say how things are or how someone feels.

ACTION VERB

I { read / am reading } a book.

Action verbs can be used in simple forms and continuous forms.

STATE VERB

I love **books.**

State verbs are not usually used in the continuous form.

5.2 FURTHER EXAMPLES ACTION AND STATE VERBS

Dominic is eating **ice cream.**

I want **to go on vacation.**

Gayle is lying **on the couch.**

She has **two cats and a dog.**

Aa 5.3 FIND EIGHT VERBS IN THE GRID AND WRITE THEM UNDER THE CORRECT HEADING

```
L O V E B I R A C S A H
T P Q A Y H E N V T Q A
R E M E M B E R D H M T
W A N T L E R E A D T E
L T B C O W D K S V X C
E E D E V T W E E E A I
L E A R N L A O E R G O
```

ACTION VERBS:

1. _____
2. _____
3. _____
4. _____

STATE VERBS:

1. _____want_____
2. _____
3. _____
4. _____

5.4 ⚠ COMMON MISTAKES STATE VERBS

It is incorrect to use state verbs in the continuous form.

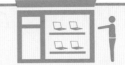

I want **a new laptop.** ✓

↑ You can usually only use
state verbs in the simple form.

I am wanting **a new laptop.** ✗

↑ You can't usually use state verbs
in the continuous form.

🔊

5.5 REWRITE THE SENTENCES, CORRECTING THE ERRORS

He **is liking** the book.
He likes the book.

❶ I **am having** a big house by the ocean.

_____

❷ My sister **is hating** this new TV show.

_____

❸ Thomas **is knowing** your dad.

_____

❹ Finn **is wanting** a new bike.

_____

❺ I **am seeing** the cat and dog.

_____

🔊

5.6 CROSS OUT THE INCORRECT WORDS IN THE SENTENCES

I **want** / ~~am wanting~~ some chocolate.

❶ She **goes** / **is going** to the store now.

❷ Fred **doesn't like** / **isn't liking** pizza.

❸ I always **sing** / **am singing** in the bath.

❹ He **reads** / **is reading** a book at the moment.

❺ Jo **remembers** / **'s remembering** my birthday.

❻ Li **plays** / **is playing** tennis at the moment.

❼ We **don't want** / **are not wanting** to leave.

🔊

---

06 Vocabulary

6.1 FEELINGS AND MOODS

calm

relaxed

happy

confident

proud

excited

surprised

pleased

cheerful

amused

irritated

angry

annoyed

furious

sad

unhappy

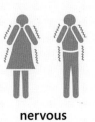
worried

lonely

scared

terrified

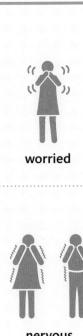
nervous

anxious

distracted

confused

disappointed

miserable

stressed

jealous

tired

bored

curious

grateful

07 | How are you feeling?

Talking about your feelings is an important part of everyday conversation. Use the present continuous to talk about how you're feeling.

⚙ New language "Feeling" and emotions
Aa Vocabulary Adjectives of emotions
🧩 New skill Talking about your feelings

TIP
"Feel" is a sta[t] verb that ca[n] be used in continuou[s] forms.

7.1 KEY LANGUAGE TALKING ABOUT YOUR FEELINGS

You can use the verb "to be" plus "feeling" to talk about your feelings.

How are you feeling?
Use "how" as the question word.

I am feeling happy.
You can use different adjectives to describe your feelings.

7.2 HOW TO FORM TALKING ABOUT YOUR FEELINGS

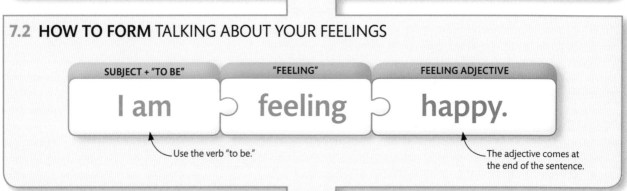

SUBJECT + "TO BE"	"FEELING"	FEELING ADJECTIVE
I am	feeling	happy.

Use the verb "to be."

The adjective comes at the end of the sentence.

7.3 FURTHER EXAMPLES TALKING ABOUT YOUR FEELINGS

I'm feeling happy.

He is feeling angry.

You are feeling proud.

She is feeling excited.

I am feeling sad.

He's feeling scared.

Aa 7.4 MATCH THE FEELINGS TO THEIR OPPOSITES

happy

bored

1 excited → sad

2 angry

miserable

3 nervous

calm

4 relaxed

confident

5 pleased

stressed

7.5 FILL IN THE GAPS TO COMPLETE THE SENTENCES

We ___*are feeling*___ nervous.

1 Ben _____ bored.

2 Luis _____ irritated.

3 I _____ sad.

4 You _____ calm.

5 Kate and I _____ happy.

6 Gina _____ confident.

7 We _____ excited.

8 I _____ tired.

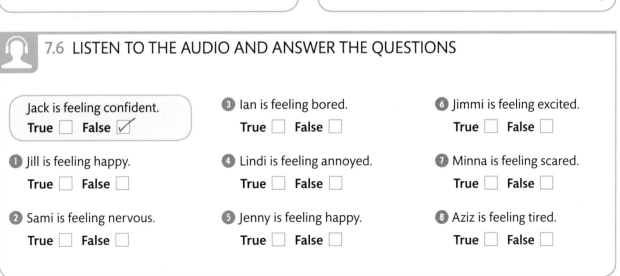

7.6 LISTEN TO THE AUDIO AND ANSWER THE QUESTIONS

Jack is feeling confident.
True ☐ **False** ☑

1 Jill is feeling happy.
True ☐ **False** ☐

2 Sami is feeling nervous.
True ☐ **False** ☐

3 Ian is feeling bored.
True ☐ **False** ☐

4 Lindi is feeling annoyed.
True ☐ **False** ☐

5 Jenny is feeling happy.
True ☐ **False** ☐

6 Jimmi is feeling excited.
True ☐ **False** ☐

7 Minna is feeling scared.
True ☐ **False** ☐

8 Aziz is feeling tired.
True ☐ **False** ☐

7.7 ANOTHER WAY TO SAY IT TALKING ABOUT YOUR FEELINGS

You can also ask how someone is, without using "feeling."

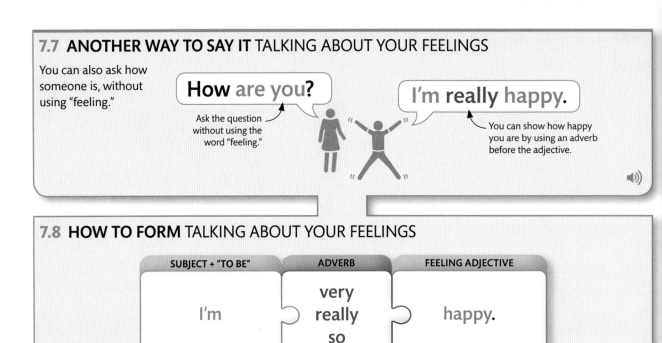

How are you?

Ask the question without using the word "feeling."

I'm really happy.

You can show how happy you are by using an adverb before the adjective.

7.8 HOW TO FORM TALKING ABOUT YOUR FEELINGS

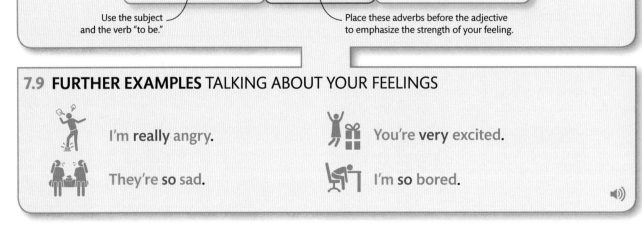

SUBJECT + "TO BE"	ADVERB	FEELING ADJECTIVE
I'm	very really so	happy.

Use the subject and the verb "to be."

Place these adverbs before the adjective to emphasize the strength of your feeling.

7.9 FURTHER EXAMPLES TALKING ABOUT YOUR FEELINGS

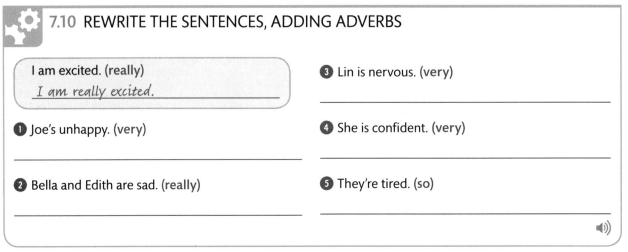

I'm **really** angry.

You're **very** excited.

They're **so** sad.

I'm **so** bored.

7.10 REWRITE THE SENTENCES, ADDING ADVERBS

I am excited. (really)

I am really excited.

❶ Joe's unhappy. (very)

_____

❷ Bella and Edith are sad. (really)

_____

❸ Lin is nervous. (very)

_____

❹ She is confident. (very)

_____

❺ They're tired. (so)

_____

I'm having a great day at the beach. All my friends are here and we're playing volleyball. I'm really ____*happy*____ .

❶ I'm at the airport. I'm waiting for the flight. I don't have a book. There's nothing to do. I'm really _____ .

❷ I'm watching a movie on TV. It's a love story. The man and his wife are in different countries. They're very _____ .

❸ We're at the concert. We're waiting for my favorite band in the world to come on stage. We're at the front. I'm so _____ .

❹ I'm at the supermarket. There's no milk, no butter, no flour, and no sugar. All the things that I need for the cake. I'm so _____ .

❺ I'm waiting to meet my new boss. She's talking to everyone in the office. I don't know what to say to her. I'm very _____ .

| sad | ~~happy~~ | bored | angry | excited | nervous |

07 ✓ CHECKLIST

⚙ "Feeling" and emotions ☐   Aa Adjectives of emotions ☐   🧩 Talking about your feelings ☐

8.1 TRANSPORTATION

car

....

taxi

....

bus

....

coach

....

plane

....

train

....

tram

....

motorcycle (US)
motorbike (UK)

....

bicycle

....

boat

....

yacht

....

ship

....

helicopter

....

bus stop

....

train station

....

taxi rank

....

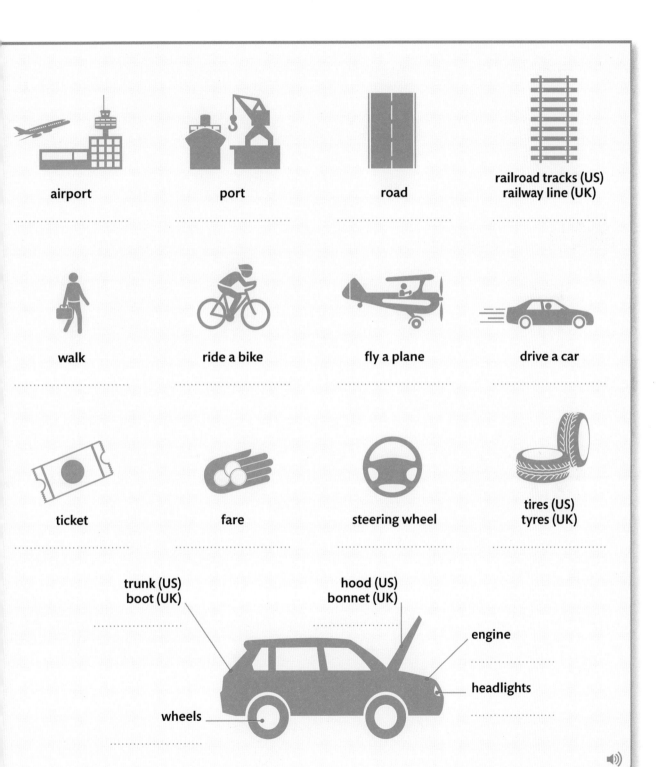

airport

port

road

railroad tracks (US)
railway line (UK)

walk

ride a bike

fly a plane

drive a car

ticket

fare

steering wheel

tires (US)
tyres (UK)

trunk (US)
boot (UK)

hood (US)
bonnet (UK)

engine

headlights

wheels

Use the present simple to describe routines, and the present continuous to say what you are doing now. These tenses are often used together.

🔧 **New language** Exceptions
Aa Vocabulary Time markers
🧩 **New skill** Contrasting routines and exceptions

9.1 KEY LANGUAGE CONTRASTING ROUTINES AND EXCEPTIONS

You can contrast a routine action with an exception to that routine by using "but."

The present simple describes something you do regularly.

This is a time marker.

I usually drive to work, but today I'm walking.

Adverbs of frequency help to show the present simple action is a routine.

Use "but" to contrast the actions.

The present continuous describes something you are doing now.

9.2 HOW TO FORM CONTRASTING ROUTINES AND EXCEPTIONS

SUBJECT	ADVERB OF FREQUENCY	VERB	"BUT"	TIME MARKER	PRESENT CONTINUOUS
I	usually mostly often	drive,	but	right now today tonight	I'm walking.

9.3 FURTHER EXAMPLES CONTRASTING ROUTINES AND EXCEPTIONS

I often stay **at home on the weekends, but** today I'm shopping **in town.**

They usually go **to the gym after work, but** tonight they're going **to the movies.**

Tonight, we're celebrating **my birthday, but** normally we don't eat **out.**

You can put the exception first.

38

9.4 FILL IN THE GAPS BY PUTTING THE VERBS IN THE CORRECT TENSES

Ben usually __*sings*__ (sing) in the school band, but today he __*is playing*__ (play) the guitar.

❶ Sarah and I normally _____ (play) tennis on Wednesdays, but today we _____ (swim).

❷ Today, I _____ (have) soup for lunch, but I usually _____ (have) a sandwich.

❸ We often _____ (watch) TV in the evenings, but tonight we _____ (have) a party.

❹ Ben and Tom usually _____ (work) until 6pm, but tonight they _____ (work) until 9pm.

❺ Melanie _____ (ski) in France this winter, but she normally _____ (go) to Italy.

❻ Today, you are _____ (drink) water, but you often _____ (have) coffee after lunch.

🔊

9.5 VOCABULARY TIME MARKERS

At the moment, **I'm knitting.**

I'm leaving right now.

I'm in a meeting this morning.

This afternoon, **we're shopping.**

Today, **I'm on vacation.**

They're seeing a play tonight.

🔊

9.6 READ THE MESSAGES AND FILL THE GAPS USING THE PRESENT CONTINUOUS

Chrissy ___*is watching a movie*___ .

① Denzel _____ .

② Selma _____ .

③ Marlow _____ .

④ Roxy _____ .

④ Rainey _____ .

⑥ Malala _____ .

⑦ Altan _____ .

Chrissy Hi everyone! I'm not studying this evening. I'm watching a movie with friends. What are you up to?

Denzel Hi! I'm seeing a show tonight. Selma was supposed to come too, but she's doing her project instead.

Marlow Hey! I'm playing hockey in the park at the moment. Can you come and play, Roxy? How about you, Rainey?

Roxy Sorry Marlow, I can't play hockey because I'm making dinner for my parents right now.

Teenie Rainey is eating with friends tonight, Marlow. But I'm bringing my hockey kit to the park right now.

Malala I'm having coffee at the moment. Altan is taking a break from work, so he's here too.

 ## 9.7 LISTEN TO THE AUDIO AND MARK WHICH ACTIVITIES ARE EXCEPTIONS

Ⓐ ☐   Ⓑ ☐   Ⓒ ☑

①

Ⓐ ☐   Ⓑ ☐   Ⓒ ☐

②

Ⓐ ☐   Ⓑ ☐   Ⓒ ☐

③

Ⓐ ☐   Ⓑ ☐   Ⓒ ☐

9.8 SAY THE SENTENCES OUT LOUD, PUTTING THE VERBS IN THE CORRECT TENSES

Phil usually ___runs___ (run), but today ___he is cycling___ (cycle).

1. Sally usually_____ (swim), but right now _____ (play) soccer.

2. Abe normally _____ (read), but tonight _____ (listen) to music.

3. They often _____ (play) golf, but today _____ (play) hockey.

4. I usually _____ (take) a shower, but today _____ (take) a bath.

09 ✓ CHECKLIST

⚙ Exceptions ☐   **Aa** Time markers ☐   🧩 Contrasting routines and exceptions ☐

↻ REVIEW THE ENGLISH YOU HAVE LEARNED IN UNITS 01–09

NEW LANGUAGE	SAMPLE SENTENCE	☑	UNIT
TALKING ABOUT YOURSELF AND YOUR DAILY ROUTINE	I am **Noah**. I'm **25 years old**. I eat **lunch at 1pm every day**.	☐	1.1, 2.1
THE PRESENT CONTINUOUS	She is wearing **a red dress**.	☐	3.1
PRESENT CONTINUOUS QUESTIONS	**What** is he **doing?**	☐	4.1
ACTION AND STATE VERBS	I am reading **a book**. I love **books**.	☐	5.1
TALKING ABOUT YOUR FEELINGS	How are you **feeling?** I am **feeling** happy.	☐	7.1
ROUTINES AND EXCEPTIONS	I usually drive **to work, but** today I'm walking.	☐	9.1

10.1 THE BODY

head	hair	face	neck
cheek	chin	shoulders	ear
eye	eyebrow	eyelashes	nose
mouth	lips	teeth	tooth

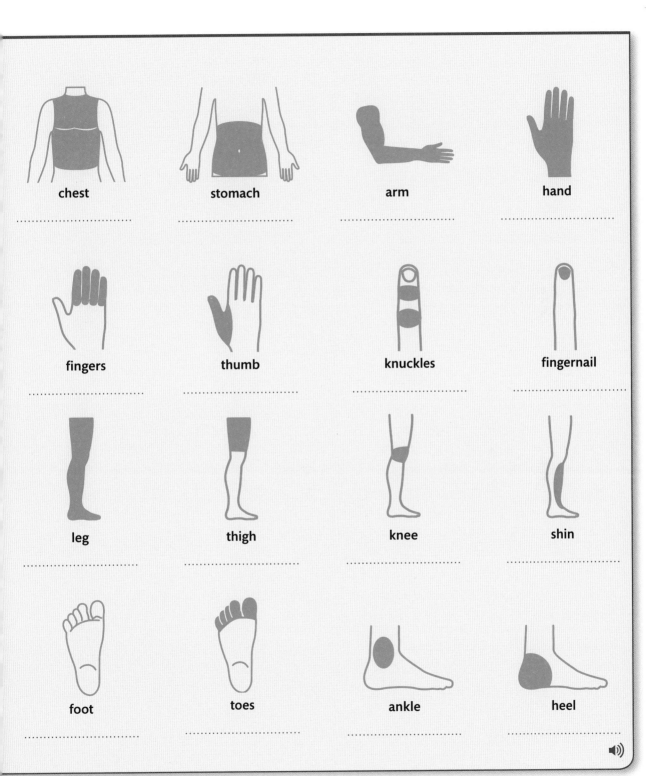

chest

stomach

arm

hand

fingers

thumb

knuckles

fingernail

leg

thigh

knee

shin

foot

toes

ankle

heel

11 What's the matter?

There are many different ways to say you're sick. You often use the negative, "not well," to talk about general illness, and "hurts," "ache," or "pain" for specific problems.

⚙ **New language** Health complaints
Aa Vocabulary Body parts and pain phrases
🧩 **New skill** Saying what's wrong

11.1 KEY LANGUAGE SAYING YOU'RE NOT FEELING WELL

To say what's wrong, use the verb "to be" with "well," "sick," or "ill." You can also use "to be" with "feeling" and an adverb to show the problem continues and to explain how bad it is.

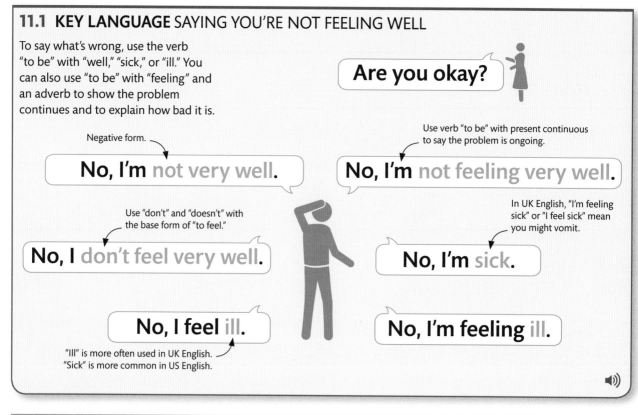

Are you okay?

Negative form.
No, I'm not very well.

Use verb "to be" with present continuous to say the problem is ongoing.
No, I'm not feeling very well.

Use "don't" and "doesn't" with the base form of "to feel."
No, I don't feel very well.

In UK English, "I'm feeling sick" or "I feel sick" mean you might vomit.
No, I'm sick.

No, I feel ill.

"Ill" is more often used in UK English. "Sick" is more common in US English.

No, I'm feeling ill.

🔊

11.2 REWRITE THE SENTENCES CORRECTING THE ERRORS

Hilary not feeling well. She's at the doctor.
Hilary's not feeling well. She's at the doctor.

① My brother isn't **feel** very well this morning.
_____

② George **are** sick, so he's staying in bed today.
_____

③ I **is** sick today, so I'm not going to work.
_____

④ Ayshah **doesn't** feeling well, so she's going home.
_____

⑤ Luca and Ben **isn't** feeling well today.
_____

🔊

11.3 KEY LANGUAGE HEALTH PROBLEMS

Use "have" and "has" with "ache," "pain," and "broken" to say what's wrong. You can also say which part of the body "hurts."

Use "have" with "broken."

I have a broken foot.
My foot hurts.

Use a part of the body with "hurts" to say where the pain is.

Use "in" with "pain" to say where it hurts.

I have a pain in my head.
I have a headache.

Headache is one word.

11.4 FURTHER EXAMPLES HEALTH PROBLEMS

She has a stomachache.

Susan's leg hurts.

You can use "got" in UK English to say what is wrong.

I've got a broken arm.

Jo has a pain in her back.

Aa 11.5 FILL IN THE GAPS USING THE WORDS IN THE PANEL

I have a bad ___headache___ .

1. Mary's back _____ .

2. John has a _____ leg.

3. I've got a _____ in my finger.

4. She has a terrible _____ .

~~headache~~   toothache   pain   broken   hurts

11.6 MARK THE SENTENCES THAT ARE CORRECT

She has a broken leg. ☑
She have a broken leg. ☐

1. I have a pain in my arm. ☐
   I am a pain in my arm. ☐

2. John has got an earache. ☐
   John has got a earache. ☐

3. He has a head hurt. ☐
   His head hurts. ☐

4. Aziz has got a pain in his back. ☐
   Aziz has got a pain on his back. ☐

11 ✓ CHECKLIST

⚙ Health complaints ☐   **Aa** Body parts and pain phrases ☐   🧩 Saying what's wrong ☐

12.1 WEATHER

cloud

fog

ice

snow

frost

sun

drizzle

rain

hail

wind

gale

storm

thunder

lightning

hurricane/
typhoon/cyclone

tornado

flood

dry

wet

humidity

temperature

warm

hot

boiling

cold

freezing

rainbow

puddle

gray sky (US)
grey sky (UK)

blue sky

12.2 WEATHER ADJECTIVES

sun ➡ sunny

cloud ➡ cloudy

fog ➡ foggy

rain ➡ rainy

snow ➡ snowy

ice ➡ icy

frost ➡ frosty

wind ➡ windy

storm ➡ stormy

thunder ➡ thundery

13 What's the weather like?

There are many ways to talk about the weather. Use the verb "to be" with weather words and phrases to describe the temperature and conditions.

⚙ **New language** Weather descriptions
Aa Vocabulary Temperature words
🧩 **New skill** Talking about the weather

13.1 KEY LANGUAGE TALKING ABOUT THE WEATHER

To ask about the weather, say: "What's the weather like?" To answer, use the verb "to be" with the correct weather word or phrase.

"Like" is a preposition here, not a verb as it is in "I like music."

What's the weather like?

Okay, but there are a lot of clouds. It's cloudy.

Use "a lot of" with a noun to show the amount of cloud.

13.2 FURTHER EXAMPLES TALKING ABOUT THE WEATHER

Beautiful! It's really hot and sunny.

Horrible! It's raining. It's wet and cold.

Use the present continuous to say what is happening with the weather now.

Really cold. It's snowing a lot and it's very icy.

There's a storm coming. It's very windy.

Aa 13.3 MATCH THE PICTURES TO THE CORRECT SENTENCES

This is a beautiful place, but I really want it to be sunny. It's dark and cloudy all the time.

1

The weather's good, and it's windy today, so we're going sailing with Sue and Louis.

2

The weather is beautiful here. It's hot and sunny, and I'm having a great time.

3

There's a lot of snow, so the children are having a great time. They want to learn how to ski.

Aa 13.4 FILL IN THE GAPS USING THE WORDS IN THE PANEL

The weather's lovely here in San Diego. It's really ___*sunny*___ .

1 Oh no! I hate this weather. It's _____ again.

2 I can't ride my bike in these conditions. It's too _____ .

3 Be careful! There's _____ on the road.

4 Wow! It's really _____ outside today.

| raining |
| ice |
| ~~sunny~~ |
| stormy |
| foggy |

13.5 KEY LANGUAGE THE TEMPERATURE

Temperature can be given in "Fahrenheit (°F)" or "Celsius (°C)." In spoken English, use the verb "to be" with a temperature phrase to talk about how hot or cold it is.

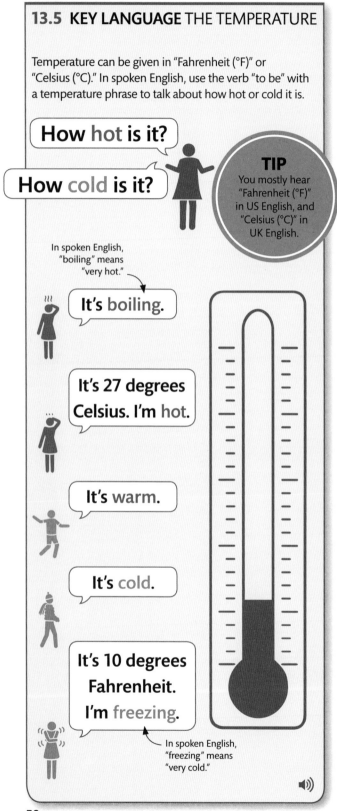

How hot is it?

How cold is it?

TIP
You mostly hear "Fahrenheit (°F)" in US English, and "Celsius (°C)" in UK English.

In spoken English, "boiling" means "very hot."

It's boiling.

It's 27 degrees Celsius. I'm hot.

It's warm.

It's cold.

It's 10 degrees Fahrenheit. I'm freezing.

In spoken English, "freezing" means "very cold."

Aa 13.6 READ THE CLUES AND WRITE THE ANSWERS IN THE CORRECT PLACES ON THE GRID

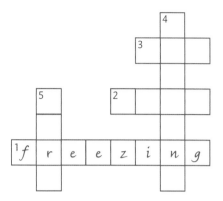

¹f r e e z i n g

ACROSS

❶ It's very cold outside. The temperature is 5°F at the moment, and I'm ___freezing___ .

❷ I'm really _____ . Can we have the heating on tonight?

❸ Sandra says it's _____ in France today. It's more than 85°F.

DOWN

❹ The sun is out and its 115°F in Turkey today. It's _____ .

❺ It's _____ outside today. Everyone's wearing T-shirts.

~~freezing~~   hot   warm
        boiling   cold

13.7 LISTEN TO THE AUDIO AND ANSWER THE QUESTIONS

A radio presenter describes the weather across North America.

Where is it 72 degrees Fahrenheit?
Kansas ☐ **Boston** ☐ **Denver** ☑

❶ What is the temperature in Calgary?
52°F ☐ **55°F** ☐ **60°F** ☐

❷ Where is there a storm at the moment?
San Francisco ☐ **Seattle** ☐ **Portland** ☐

❸ Where is there snow today?
Vancouver ☐ **Edmonton** ☐ **Anchorage** ☐

❹ Where are there no clouds?
Phoenix ☐ **Houston** ☐ **Dallas** ☐

13.8 WRITE EACH SENTENCE IN ITS OTHER FORM

There's a lot of fog.
It's very foggy.

❶ It's very icy.
_____

❷ There's a lot of wind.
_____

❸ There's a lot of rain.
_____

❹ The sun is shining.
_____

❺ It's very cloudy.
_____

---

13 ✔ CHECKLIST

⚙ Weather descriptions ☐   **Aa** Temperature words ☐   Talking about the weather ☐

🔄 REVIEW THE ENGLISH YOU HAVE LEARNED IN UNITS 11-13

NEW LANGUAGE	SAMPLE SENTENCE	☑	UNIT
SAYING YOU'RE NOT FEELING WELL	**Are you okay? No, I'm** not feeling very well.	☐	11.1
HEALTH PROBLEMS	**I have a** broken foot. **My foot** hurts. **I have a** pain **in my head. I have a** headache.	☐	11.3, 11.4
TALKING ABOUT THE WEATHER	**What's the weather like? Okay, but there are** a lot of clouds. **It's** cloudy.	☐	13.1, 13.2
GIVING THE TEMPERATURE	It's 27 degrees celsius. It's 10 degrees fahrenheit.	☐	13.5
TEMPERATURE PHRASES	**How hot is it? It's** boiling. **How cold is it. It's** freezing.	☐	13.5

14.1 TRAVEL

late

on time

pack your bags

luggage

arrive at the airport

terminal

check-in

boarding card

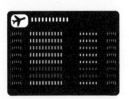

flight

hand luggage

security

delay

board a plane

fly in a plane

land at the airport

passport control

miss a flight

runway

set off on a journey

road trip

visit a museum

go sightseeing

get on a bus

get off a bus

hotel

apartment

hostel

cruise

arrive at a hotel

reception

stay in a hotel

leave a hotel

15 Making comparisons

A comparative adjective is used to describe the difference between two nouns. Use it before the word "than" to compare people, places, or things.

⚙ **New language** Comparative adjectives
Aa Vocabulary Travel and countries
🧩 **New skill** Comparing things

15.1 KEY LANGUAGE COMPARATIVE ADJECTIVES

For most adjectives with one or two syllables, add "er" to make the comparative.

Greece is warm.

Greece is warmer than France.

Add "er" to make the comparative.

Use "than" after the comparative adjective.

🔊

15.2 FURTHER EXAMPLES COMPARATIVE ADJECTIVES

 Ahmed is taller than Jonathan.

 A plane is faster than a train.

 5°F is colder than 85°F.

Sanjay is younger than Tina.

🔊

15.3 KEY LANGUAGE FORMING COMPARATIVES

There are special rules for adjectives ending in "e," "y," and with a single consonant.

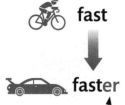 **fast**

 **faster**

Add "er" to most adjectives of one or two syllables.

close

closer

If the adjective ends in "e," just add "r."

 early

 earlier

For some adjectives ending in "y," take off the "y" and add "ier."

 **big**

 bigger

For single-syllable adjectives ending consonant-vowel-consonant, double the final letter and add "er."

🔊

15.4 FILL IN THE GAPS USING THE WORDS IN THE PANEL TO COMPLETE THE SENTENCES

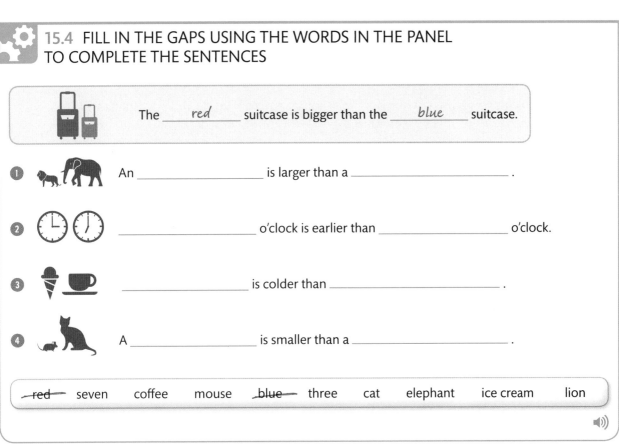

The _____red_____ suitcase is bigger than the _____blue_____ suitcase.

1. An _____ is larger than a _____ .

2. _____ o'clock is earlier than _____ o'clock.

3. _____ is colder than _____ .

4. A _____ is smaller than a _____ .

red   seven   coffee   mouse   blue   three   cat   elephant   ice cream   lion

Aa 15.5 FIND NINE COMPARATIVES IN THE GRID AND WRITE THEM NEXT TO THE CORRECT ADJECTIVE

```
E R P W T I E V E H C L
H V K K R K N I A I F O
O H M E A S I E R G V W
T L A T E R C Y L H F E
T Y T X E L I C I E Q R
E F L A R G E R E R L T
R K T H I N N E R E V K
J A K I O H M R N P L Q
G D H B C L O S E R E D
```

thin	=	_thinner_
1 low	=	_____
2 high	=	_____
3 large	=	_____
4 late	=	_____
5 easy	=	_____
6 early	=	_____
7 hot	=	_____
8 close	=	_____

15.6 KEY LANGUAGE COMPARATIVES WITH LONG ADJECTIVES

For some two-syllable adjectives and those of three syllables or more, use "more" and "than" to make the comparative.

This beach is beautiful.

The adjective "beautiful" has three syllables, so you say "more beautiful than."

This beach is more beautiful than that one.

Use "more" before the adjective.

Use "than" after the adjective.

15.7 HOW TO FORM COMPARATIVES WITH LONG ADJECTIVES

SUBJECT + VERB	"MORE"	ADJECTIVE	"THAN"	REST OF SENTENCE
This beach is	more	beautiful	than	that one.

15.8 FURTHER EXAMPLES COMPARATIVES WITH LONG ADJECTIVES

 Surfing is more exciting than **going to the gym.**

 This book is more interesting than **that one.**

 Flying is more expensive than **traveling by car.**

 For me, science is more difficult than **history.**

15.9 FILL IN THE GAPS USING THE CORRECT COMPARATIVES

This movie is really exciting. It's _____*more exciting than*_____ the book.

1 The Hotel Supreme is very expensive. It's _____ the Motel Excelsior.

2 The physics exam is really difficult. It's _____ the biology exam.

3 Your dress is very beautiful. It's _____ my dress.

4 This TV program is really interesting. It's _____ the other ones.

15.10 FILL IN THE GAPS BY PUTTING THE ADJECTIVES INTO THEIR COMPARATIVE FORMS

The balloon is _____*lighter than*_____ (light) the birthday cake.

1. This laptop is _____ (expensive) this phone.

2. Seven o'clock is _____ (late) three o'clock.

3. A game of chess is _____ (difficult) a game of cards.

4. A horse is _____ (big) a rabbit.

15.11 LISTEN TO THE AUDIO AND ANSWER THE QUESTIONS

Selma and Joe are deciding where to go on vacation.

Costa Rica is hotter than the Bahamas.
True ☑ False ☐

1. The Bahamas is easier to fly to than Costa Rica.
True ☐ False ☐

2. The Bahamas is more expensive than Costa Rica.
True ☐ False ☐

3. Tahiti Beach is more beautiful than Playa Hermosa.
True ☐ False ☐

4. Joe thinks the Bahamas is more exciting than Costa Rica.
True ☐ False ☐

15.12 CROSS OUT THE INCORRECT WORDS IN EACH SENTENCE

An elephant is bigger / more big than a lion.

1. Paris is beautiful / more beautiful than Dallas.

2. Noon is earlier / more early than 5pm.

3. A cheetah is faster / more fast than a bear.

4. Gold is expensive / more expensive than silver.

5. Rock is harder / more hard than paper.

6. Water is warmer / more warm than ice.

7. Skiing is exciting / more exciting than walking.

15 ✓ CHECKLIST

⚙ Comparative adjectives ☐   Aa Travel and countries ☐   🧩 Comparing things ☐

16 Talking about extremes

Use superlative adjectives to talk about extremes, such as "the biggest" or "the smallest." For long adjectives, use "the most" to make the superlative.

⚙ **New language** Superlative adjectives
Aa Vocabulary Animals, facts, and places
🧩 **New skill** Talking about extremes

16.1 KEY LANGUAGE SUPERLATIVE ADJECTIVES

For most adjectives with one or two syllables, add "est" to make the superlative.

The comparative describes the difference between two things.

K2 is higher than Annapurna, but Everest is the highest mountain in the world.

Always use the definite article ("the") before the superlative.

The superlative describes which thing is the most extreme.

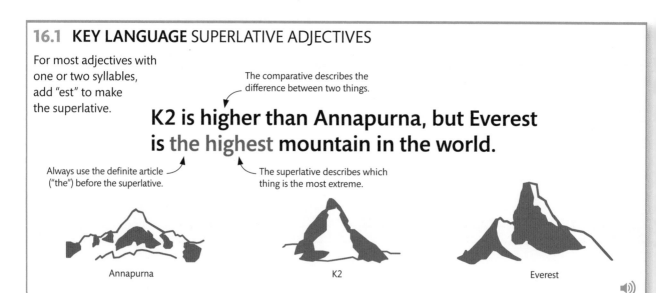

Annapurna   K2   Everest

16.2 FURTHER EXAMPLES SUPERLATIVE ADJECTIVES

Rhinos are bigger than cows, but elephants are the biggest land animals.

Great white sharks are larger than dolphins, but blue whales are the largest animals in the world.

16.3 HOW TO FORM SENTENCES WITH SUPERLATIVES

SUBJECT + VERB	"THE" + SUPERLATIVE	REST OF SENTENCE
K2 is	the highest	mountain in the world.

16.4 KEY LANGUAGE FORMING SUPERLATIVES

There are special rules for adjectives ending in "e" or "y," and for some that end with a single consonant.

fast → **fastest**
Add "est" to most adjectives of one or two syllables.

close → **closest**
If the adjective ends in "e," you just add "st."

early → **earliest**
For some adjectives ending in "y," take off the "y" and add "iest."

big → **biggest**
For single-syllable adjectives ending consonant-vowel-consonant, double the final letter and add "est."

16.5 LISTEN TO THE AUDIO AND ANSWER THE QUESTIONS

Friends Joel, Sarah, and Ben talk about the things they've bought.

Who has the fastest car?
Joel ☐ Sarah ✓ Ben ☐

1 Who is the tallest?
Joel ☐ Sarah ☐ Ben ☐

2 Who has the smallest phone?
Joel ☐ Sarah ☐ Ben ☐

3 Who has the cheapest laptop?
Joel ☐ Sarah ☐ Ben ☐

4 Who has the most expensive apartment?
Joel ☐ Sarah ☐ Ben ☐

5 Who is the youngest?
Joel ☐ Sarah ☐ Ben ☐

16.6 FILL IN THE GAPS BY PUTTING THE ADJECTIVES IN THE CORRECT FORM

The _____oldest_____ (old) plane in the world is the Blériot XI.

1 The African elephant is the _____ (heavy) animal on land.

2 The _____ (fast) animal in the world is the peregrine falcon.

3 The _____ (long) word in the English dictionary has 45 letters.

4 The Sahara is the _____ (big) desert in the world.

5 The giraffe is the _____ (tall) animal on Earth.

16.7 KEY LANGUAGE SUPERLATIVES WITH LONG ADJECTIVES

For some two-syllable adjectives and for adjectives of three syllables or more,
use "the most" before the adjective. The form of the adjective doesn't change.

$ $$ $$$

The Palace Hotel is more expensive than the Rialto, but the Biaritz is the most expensive hotel in the city.

Use "the most" with the adjective.   The adjective stays the same.

16.8 HOW TO FORM SUPERLATIVES WITH LONG ADJECTIVES

SUBJECT + VERB	"THE" + SUPERLATIVE	ADJECTIVE	REST OF SENTENCE
This is	the most	expensive	hotel in the city.

16.9 FURTHER EXAMPLES SUPERLATIVES WITH LONG ADJECTIVES

The science museum is the most interesting museum in town.

The Twister is the most exciting ride in the theme park.

This is the most comfortable chair in the room.

16.10 MATCH THE BEGINNINGS OF THE SENTENCES TO THE CORRECT ENDINGS

The Yangtze River is   the largest state in the US.

❶ Antarctica is   the coldest place on Earth.

❷ Mumbai is   the most dangerous snake in the world.

❸ Alaska is   the longest river in Asia.

❹ The inland taipan is   the biggest city in India.

16.11 READ THE ARTICLE AND ANSWER THE QUESTIONS

The Hotel Blog
HOME | ENTRIES | ABOUT | CONTACT

POSTED FRIDAY, 28 AUGUST

The Rialto (height: 500 feet) is two miles from the beach. The average temperature is a hot 85°F, and it's in a three-star (***) area of natural beauty. *Room per night: $500. Number of rooms: 300.*

The Plaza (height: 600 feet) is one mile from the beach, and in a five-star (*****) area of natural beauty. The temperature is usually a warm 75°F. *Room per night: $400. Number of rooms: 500.*

The Grand (height: 300 feet) is less than a mile from the beach. It's in a four-star (****) area of natural beauty, and the temperature is a cool 65°F. *Room per night: $515. Number of rooms: 200.*

Which is the most expensive hotel?
The Rialto ☐ **The Plaza** ☐ **The Grand** ☑

1 Which hotel is the closest to the beach?
The Rialto ☐ **The Plaza** ☐ **The Grand** ☐

2 Which is the tallest hotel?
The Rialto ☐ **The Plaza** ☐ **The Grand** ☐

3 Which hotel is in the most beautiful area?
The Rialto ☐ **The Plaza** ☐ **The Grand** ☐

4 Which hotel has the fewest rooms?
The Rialto ☐ **The Plaza** ☐ **The Grand** ☐

5 Which hotel is in the warmest place?
The Rialto ☐ **The Plaza** ☐ **The Grand** ☐

16.12 SAY THE SENTENCES OUT LOUD, FILLING IN THE GAPS USING SUPERLATIVES

Mount Everest is a very high mountain. It is ___*the highest*___ mountain in the world.

1 Istanbul is a very large city. It is _____ city in Europe.

2 The Missouri River is 2,540 miles long. It is _____ river in North America.

3 The cheetah is a very fast animal. It is _____ land animal on Earth.

4 The Kali Gandaki Gorge is 3.46 miles deep. It is _____ gorge in the world.

16 ✓ CHECKLIST

⚙ Superlative adjectives ☐   **Aa** Animals, facts, and places ☐   🧩 Talking about extremes ☐

17 | Vocabulary

17.1 GEOGRAPHICAL FEATURES

ocean

sea

coast

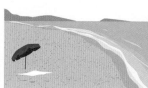

beach

island

cliff

rock

cave

waterfall

countryside

field

hill

mountain

valley

canyon

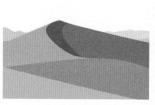

sand dune

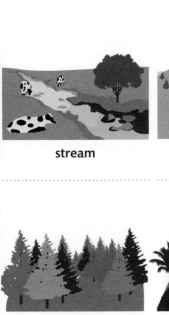

stream

river

pond

lake

woods

jungle

rainforest

swamp

desert

oasis

volcano

polar region

glacier

iceberg

18 Making choices

"Which," "what," "and," and "or" are all useful words to add to questions. You can use them to show whether a question is general or about specific options.

⚙ **New language** "Which" and "what"
Aa Vocabulary Geographical words
🧩 **New skill** Asking multiple-choice questions

18.1 KEY LANGUAGE "AND / OR"

Use "and" to ask about more than one thing, and "or" for choices and alternatives.

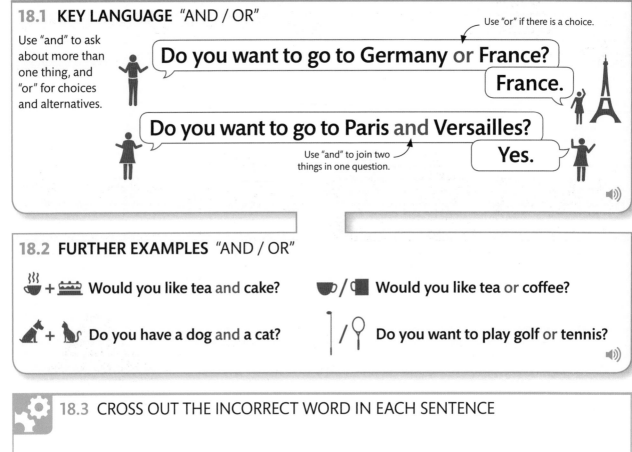

Use "or" if there is a choice.

Do you want to go to Germany or France?

France.

Do you want to go to Paris and Versailles?

Use "and" to join two things in one question.

Yes.

18.2 FURTHER EXAMPLES "AND / OR"

Would you like tea and cake?

Would you like tea or coffee?

Do you have a dog and a cat?

Do you want to play golf or tennis?

18.3 CROSS OUT THE INCORRECT WORD IN EACH SENTENCE

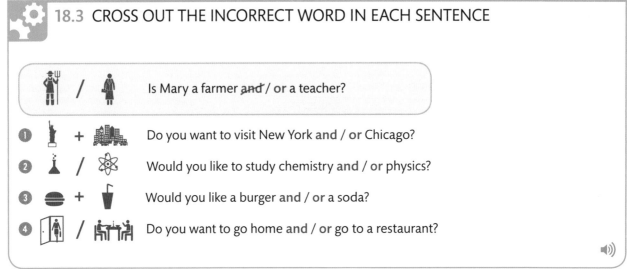

Is Mary a farmer and̶ / or a teacher?

1. Do you want to visit New York and / or Chicago?

2. Would you like to study chemistry and / or physics?

3. Would you like a burger and / or a soda?

4. Do you want to go home and / or go to a restaurant?

18.4 KEY LANGUAGE "WHICH / WHAT"

You use "which" when there are two or more possibilities in the question. Use "what" when the question is more general.

There are no choices in the question.

What is the tallest building in the world?

The question includes a choice of possible answers.

Which building is taller, Big Ben or the Eiffel Tower?

18.5 FURTHER EXAMPLES "WHICH / WHAT"

What is the highest mountain in the Himalayas?

What is the fastest animal in the world?

Which mountain is higher, the Matterhorn or Mont Blanc?

Which animal is the fastest, a lion, a rhino, or a cheetah?

18.6 FILL IN THE GAPS USING "WHICH" OR "WHAT"

_____*Which*_____ country would you like to visit, India, China, or Thailand?

❶ _____ is the biggest country in Africa?

❷ _____ would you like to eat for your dinner?

❸ _____ jacket do you want to wear, the blue one or the red one?

❹ _____ is your favorite color, red, green, yellow, or blue?

18.7 KEY LANGUAGE IRREGULAR COMPARATIVES AND SUPERLATIVES

Some common adjectives have irregular comparatives and superlatives.

ADJECTIVE	COMPARATIVE	SUPERLATIVE
good	better	best
bad	worse	worst
far	farther (US) / further (UK)	farthest (US) / furthest (UK)

TIP
In US English, "further" and "furthest" are used to describe figurative (not physical) distances.

18.8 FURTHER EXAMPLES IRREGULAR COMPARATIVES AND SUPERLATIVES

The tree is far **away.**

The house is farther **away than the tree.**

The mountain is the farthest **away.**

John got a good **grade on his exam.**

Jill got a better **grade than John.**

Aziz got the best **grade.**

New York has bad **weather today.**

Paris has worse **weather.**

London has the worst **weather.**

18.9 READ THE ARTICLE AND ANSWER THE QUESTIONS

Which restaurant has the best service?

The Little Olive has the best service.

1 Which has the best music?

_____

2 Which is the farthest from the beach?

_____

3 Which has the best ice cream?

_____

4 Which has the worst food?

_____

5 Which has the best seafood?

_____

PLACES TO EAT
Where to go for dinner this weekend

THE LITTLE OLIVE – This restaurant is five minutes from the beach. It has no live music, but the food is great and its seafood is the best in town. The service here is excellent.

JOHN'S BAR – This is a great place to listen to music. It's on the beach and has bands every night. The food and service are OK.

SEAVIEW CAFÉ – This café is two minutes from the beach. It doesn't have music, but the food and service aren't bad. Go here for the ice cream, it's the best in town.

THE BIG CAHUNA – They play OK music here, but the food and service are not good. It's more than ten minutes from the beach, but it has the best views in town.

18.10 LISTEN TO THE AUDIO AND ANSWER THE QUESTIONS

Rita Adams answers questions on a TV game show.

Which is the largest US state?
Texas ☐ **Virginia** ☐ **Alaska** ☑

1 Which city is farthest from the equator?
Taipei ☐ **Bangkok** ☐ **Manila** ☐

2 Which is the smallest South American country?
Brazil ☐ **Peru** ☐ **Suriname** ☐

3 Which is the biggest desert?
Mojave ☐ **Sahara** ☐ **Kalahari** ☐

4 Which is the tallest building?
Big Ben ☐ **Eiffel Tower** ☐ **Pisa Tower** ☐

5 Which is the highest mountain?
K2 ☐ **Kilimanjaro** ☐ **Mont Blanc** ☐

---

18 ✓ CHECKLIST

⚙ "Which" and "what" ☐   **Aa** Geographical words ☐   🧩 Asking multiple-choice questions ☐

19 Using large numbers

You usually write numbers larger than 100 in figures. To say them, add "and" in front of the number signified by the last two digits, such as "one hundred and ten."

⚙ **New language** Large numbers
Aa Vocabulary Thousands and millions
🧩 **New skill** Talking about large amounts

19.1 KEY LANGUAGE LARGE NUMBERS

You can say "one hundred" or "a hundred." Both are correct. Don't add "s" to "hundred," "thousand," or "million."

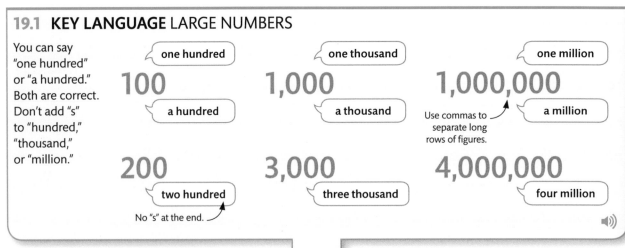

one hundred
100
a hundred

one thousand
1,000
a thousand

one million
1,000,000
a million

Use commas to separate long rows of figures.

200
two hundred
No "s" at the end.

3,000
three thousand

4,000,000
four million

19.2 FURTHER EXAMPLES LARGE NUMBERS

Add "and" before the last two numbers to say numbers higher than one hundred.

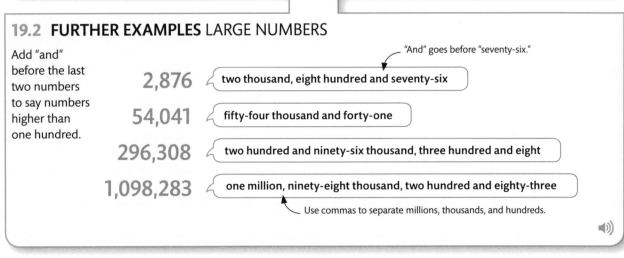

"And" goes before "seventy-six."

2,876 — two thousand, eight hundred and seventy-six

54,041 — fifty-four thousand and forty-one

296,308 — two hundred and ninety-six thousand, three hundred and eight

1,098,283 — one million, ninety-eight thousand, two hundred and eighty-three

Use commas to separate millions, thousands, and hundreds.

19.3 LISTEN TO THE AUDIO AND MARK THE NUMBERS YOU HEAR

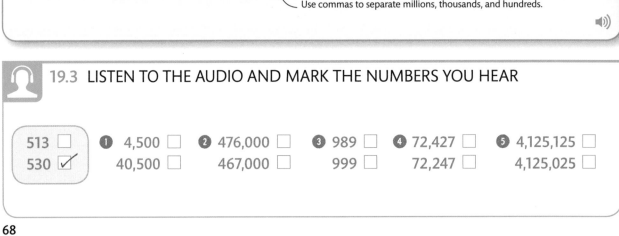

513 ☐
530 ✓

1 4,500 ☐
   40,500 ☐

2 476,000 ☐
   467,000 ☐

3 989 ☐
   999 ☐

4 72,427 ☐
   72,247 ☐

5 4,125,125 ☐
   4,125,025 ☐

19.4 SAY THE NUMBERS OUT LOUD

532	*five hundred and thirty-two*

1 3,107

2 23,417

3 345,972

4 23,456,987

---

19 ✓ CHECKLIST

⚙ Large numbers ☐   **Aa** Thousands and millions ☐   🧩 Talking about large amounts ☐

↻ REVIEW THE ENGLISH YOU HAVE LEARNED IN UNITS 15-19

NEW LANGUAGE	SAMPLE SENTENCE	☑	UNIT
COMPARATIVE ADJECTIVES	Greece is warmer than France.	☐	15.1, 15.3, 15.6
SUPERLATIVE ADJECTIVES	K2 is higher than Annapurna, but Everest is the highest mountain in the world.	☐	16.1, 16.4, 16.7
"AND" AND "OR"	Do you want to go to Germany or France? Do you want to go to Paris and Versailles?	☐	18.1, 18.2
"WHICH" AND "WHAT"	What is the tallest building? Which mountain is higher, the Matterhorn or Mont Blanc?	☐	18.4, 18.5
LARGE NUMBERS	Two thousand, eight hundred and seventy-six	☐	19.1, 19.2

20.1 THE CALENDAR

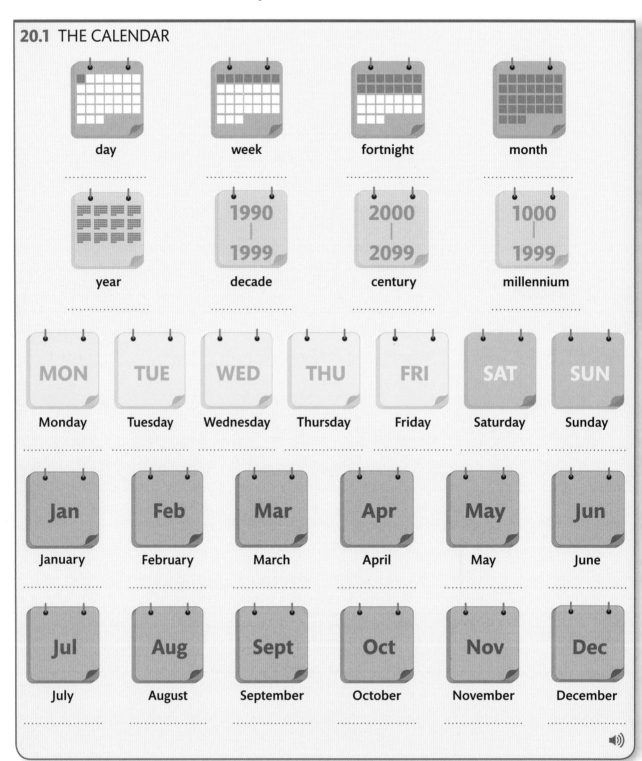

day

week

fortnight

month

year

decade

century

millennium

MON Monday

TUE Tuesday

WED Wednesday

THU Thursday

FRI Friday

SAT Saturday

SUN Sunday

Jan January

Feb February

Mar March

Apr April

May May

Jun June

Jul July

Aug August

Sept September

Oct October

Nov November

Dec December

20.2 SEASONS

spring

summer

fall (US)
autumn (UK)

winter

20.3 ORDINAL NUMBERS

1st first	**2nd** second	**3rd** third	**4th** fourth
5th fifth	**6th** sixth	**7th** seventh	**8th** eighth
9th ninth	**10th** tenth	**11th** eleventh	**12th** twelfth
13th thirteenth	**14th** fourteenth	**15th** fifteenth	**16th** sixteenth
17th seventeenth	**18th** eighteenth	**19th** nineteenth	**20th** twentieth
21st twenty-first	**22nd** twenty-second	**23rd** twenty-third	**24th** twenty-fourth
25th twenty-fifth	**26th** twenty-sixth	**27th** twenty-seventh	**28th** twenty-eighth
29th twenty-ninth	**30th** thirtieth	**31st** thirty-first	

21 Talking about dates

There are two different ways of writing and saying dates. You use numbers along with the month to define the date you're talking about.

⚙ **New language** Dates, "was born," "ago"
Aa Vocabulary Numbers, months, and years
🧩 **New skill** Talking about dates

21.1 KEY LANGUAGE WRITING AND SAYING DATES

In the US, people often describe dates by writing cardinal numbers and saying ordinal numbers.

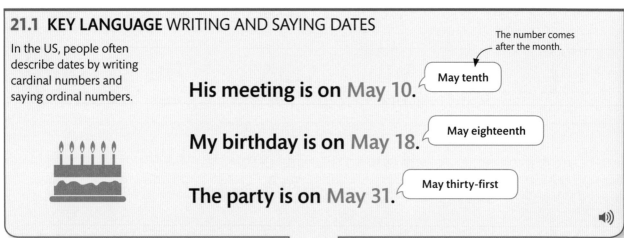

The number comes after the month.

His meeting is on May 10. _May tenth_

My birthday is on May 18. _May eighteenth_

The party is on May 31. _May thirty-first_

21.2 ANOTHER WAY TO SAY IT WRITING AND SAYING DATES

In some other places, such as the UK, people use ordinal numbers to write and say dates.

His meeting is on the 10th of May. _the tenth of May_

My birthday is on May the 18th. _May the eighteenth_

The party is on the 31st of May. _the thirty-first of May_

21.3 LISTEN TO THE AUDIO, THEN NUMBER THE DATES IN THE ORDER THEY ARE DISCUSSED

Ⓐ November 17 ☐   Ⓑ March 22 ① Ⓒ September 13 ☐   Ⓓ May 19 ☐

Ⓔ August 31 ☐   Ⓕ April 5 ☐   Ⓖ June 5 ☐

21.4 KEY LANGUAGE USING "WAS BORN"

Use "was born" to talk about someone's date or year of birth.

Jim was born in { 1975. 2015.

nineteen seventy-five

twenty fifteen

You say most dates by grouping the date into pairs of numbers, such as "nineteen" and "seventy-five."

You can say "two thousand and fifteen" or "twenty fifteen."

21.5 KEY LANGUAGE USING "AGO"

You use "ago" to say how many years before now something happened.

Plato was born around 2,500 years ago, in 424 BCE.

"Ago" means "before now."

21.6 LISTEN TO THE AUDIO AND NOTE THE YEAR OF EACH EVENT

  ❶ ❷ ❸ ❹ ❺

1971 _____ _____ _____ _____

21.7 USE THE CHART TO CREATE 12 CORRECT SENTENCES AND SAY THEM OUT LOUD

My birthday is on December 5.

| My / Nami's / I / He | birthday / meeting | is on | December 5. / the 11th of March. |
| | was born | 20 / 41 | years ago. |

22 Talking about the past

The past simple describes events that happened at a definite time in the past, or the state of things at a particular point in time.

⚙️ **New language** The past simple of "to be"
Aa Vocabulary Jobs, town, and life events
🧩 **New skill** Talking about past states

22.1 KEY LANGUAGE THE PAST SIMPLE OF "TO BE"

Any action that happened and was completed in the past can be described in the past simple. The past simple of "to be" is "was" or "were."

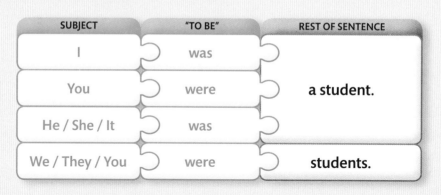

This is the present simple.

Jill is a businesswoman now.

She was a student in 1985.

This is the past simple.

This is a definite time in the past.

🔊

22.2 HOW TO FORM THE PAST SIMPLE OF "TO BE"

The past simple of "to be" changes with the subject.

SUBJECT	"TO BE"	REST OF SENTENCE
I	was	
You	were	a student.
He / She / It	was	
We / They / You	were	students.

22.3 FURTHER EXAMPLES THE PAST SIMPLE OF "TO BE"

He was **a doctor for 40 years.**

We were **at the library yesterday.**

She was **a Broadway star in the 1960s.**

There were **lots of people at the party.**

There was **a party last night.**

They were **at the movies last week.**

🔊

22.4 CROSS OUT THE INCORRECT WORD IN EACH SENTENCE

She was / were a teacher.

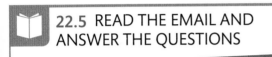

1. You was / were at the museum last week.

2. There was / were five people here yesterday.

3. The students was / were there on Monday morning.

4. My mom was / were an artist in the 1990s.

5. I was / were in college in 1989.

6. Sal and I was / were at the theater last night.

7. My dad was / were a builder until 1995.

22.5 READ THE EMAIL AND ANSWER THE QUESTIONS

∨ ✕

⊠

To: Jules

Subject: Weekend in L.A.

How are you? I was in Los Angeles on the weekend. I was at Manhattan Beach. Do you know it? It was very hot and there were lots of people there. There are many cafés there, too. I was in a café called Ocean View and Malcolm was there. He was with a woman called Stacey. Is she his girlfriend?....

Annie x

↩ ↩↩   𝓞 🗑

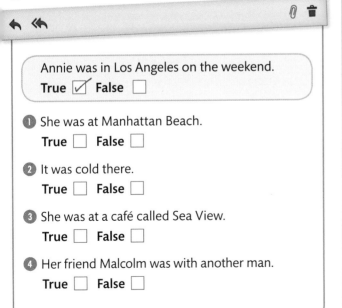

Annie was in Los Angeles on the weekend.
True ☑ **False** ☐

1. She was at Manhattan Beach.
True ☐ **False** ☐

2. It was cold there.
True ☐ **False** ☐

3. She was at a café called Sea View.
True ☐ **False** ☐

4. Her friend Malcolm was with another man.
True ☐ **False** ☐

22.6 LISTEN TO THE AUDIO AND MATCH THE EVENTS TO THE YEARS

Chat Radio give the answers to their "That Was The Day" quiz.

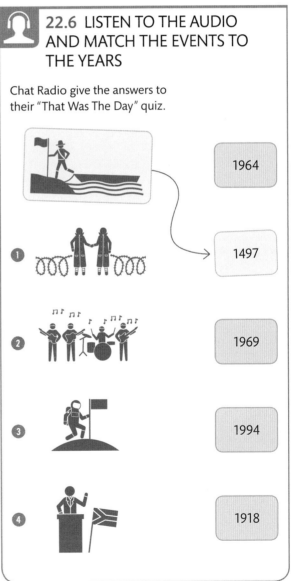

75

22.7 KEY LANGUAGE "WAS" / "WERE" NEGATIVES

As in the present simple, use "not" to form negative statements in the past simple.

Add "not" after "was" or "were."

He $\left\{ \begin{array}{c} \text{was not} \\ \text{wasn't} \end{array} \right\}$ a teacher in 2004.

They $\left\{ \begin{array}{c} \text{were not} \\ \text{weren't} \end{array} \right\}$ at the park yesterday.

You can contract these negatives to their short forms.

22.8 KEY LANGUAGE "WAS" / "WERE" QUESTIONS

To ask questions about the past using the verb "to be," swap the subject and verb.

He was in India.

Was he in India?

Swap the subject and "to be."

They were late for school.

Were they late for school?

22.9 FURTHER EXAMPLES "WAS" / "WERE" NEGATIVES AND QUESTIONS

I wasn't **a good waiter.**

There weren't **any boats.**

Were there **any cakes at the party?**

Was he **good at playing tennis?**

22.10 CROSS OUT THE INCORRECT WORD IN EACH SENTENCE

He wasn't / ~~weren't~~ a doctor.

1 They wasn't / weren't very good at science.

2 I wasn't / weren't in Canada in 2002.

3 You wasn't / weren't at the party last night.

4 We wasn't / weren't in our house last year.

5 There wasn't / weren't a restaurant near the river.

22.11 WRITE QUESTIONS BASED ON THE STATEMENTS

There were some factories.
Were there any factories?

1 He was a good builder.
_____

2 They were late this morning.
_____

3 She was at a meeting yesterday.
_____

4 You were happy in college.
_____

5 We were in New Zealand for two weeks.
_____

6 You were in the swimming pool.
_____

22.12 LISTEN TO THE AUDIO AND MARK WHAT EACH BUILDING WAS USED FOR IN THE PAST

A tour guide is talking about the history of some old buildings.

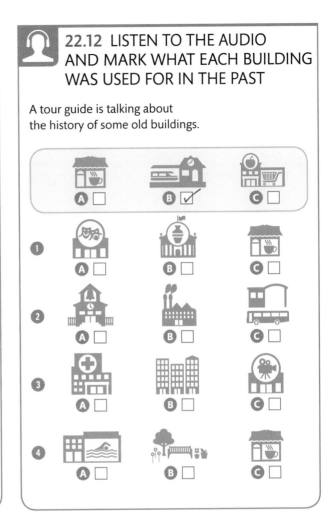

22.13 USE THE CHART TO CREATE 15 CORRECT SENTENCES AND SAY THEM OUT LOUD

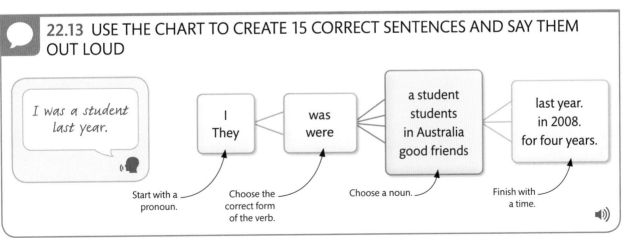

I was a student last year.

| I / They | was / were | a student / students / in Australia / good friends | last year. / in 2008. / for four years. |

Start with a pronoun.
Choose the correct form of the verb.
Choose a noun.
Finish with a time.

22 ✓ CHECKLIST

⚙ The past simple of "to be" ☐   Aa Jobs, town, and life events ☐   🧩 Talking about past states ☐

23 Past events

Some verbs are regular in the past simple. You can use a lot of them to talk about the past week, the last year, or your life. Their past simple forms ends in "-ed."

⚙ **New language** Regular verbs in the past simple
Aa Vocabulary Pastimes and life events
🧩 **New skill** Talking about your past

23.1 KEY LANGUAGE REGULAR VERBS IN THE PAST SIMPLE

The past simple describes events that happened in the past. The past simple forms of regular verbs end in "-ed." The negative uses "did not" plus the base form.

The verb ends in "-ed."

I visited Luke last Friday.

He didn't play tennis last night.

23.2 HOW TO FORM REGULAR VERBS IN THE PAST SIMPLE

The past forms of most verbs do not change with the subject. Use the past simple of "do" plus the base verb to form negative statements.

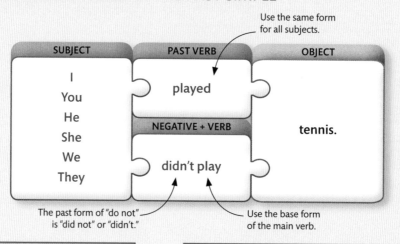

Use the same form for all subjects.

SUBJECT	PAST VERB	OBJECT
I You He She We They	played	tennis.
	NEGATIVE + VERB	
	didn't play	

The past form of "do not" is "did not" or "didn't."

Use the base form of the main verb.

23.3 FURTHER EXAMPLES REGULAR VERBS IN THE PAST SIMPLE

Questions are formed using "did" + subject + the base form of the verb.

He walked to the office.

She didn't walk downtown.

Did they work late?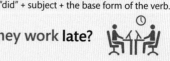

We didn't watch TV today.

23.4 FILL IN THE GAPS BY PUTTING THE VERBS IN THE PAST SIMPLE

Last Friday, I _____*cooked*_____ (cook) a meal for my friends.

1. The music was good, but I _____ (not dance) very much.

2. My friend _____ (not listen) to the band on Saturday night.

3. Last week, I _____ (clean) my brother's new car for him.

4. Did you _____ (watch) a fun movie last night?

5. Ben and Franklin _____ (play) tennis for five hours yesterday.

23.5 KEY LANGUAGE SPELLING RULES FOR THE PAST SIMPLE

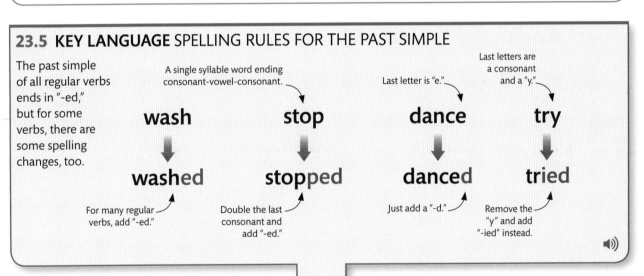

The past simple of all regular verbs ends in "-ed," but for some verbs, there are some spelling changes, too.

A single syllable word ending consonant-vowel-consonant.

Last letter is "e."

Last letters are a consonant and a "y."

wash → **washed**
For many regular verbs, add "-ed."

stop → **stopped**
Double the last consonant and add "-ed."

dance → **danced**
Just add a "-d."

try → **tried**
Remove the "y" and add "-ied" instead.

23.6 FURTHER EXAMPLES SPELLING RULES FOR THE PAST SIMPLE

He carried **the bags for her.**

We arrived **here at midnight.**

I studied **English last year.**

They saved **money for a vacation.**

23.7 LOOK AT JOYCE'S DIARY FROM LAST WEEK AND FILL IN THE GAPS TO COMPLETE THE SENTENCES

WEEKLY PLANNER

MONDAY
Evening: watch movie on TV

TUESDAY
Morning: play squash
Afternoon: phone my boss

WEDNESDAY
try sushi at Japanese restaurant

THURSDAY
Morning: clean the bathroom
Night: visit Aziz in hospital

FRIDAY
invite friends to my birthday party

SATURDAY
walk in the park

SUNDAY
cook dinner for my parents

On Monday evening, Joyce ___*watched*___ a movie on TV.

1 On Tuesday morning, she _____ squash.

2 On Tuesday afternoon, she _____ her boss.

3 On Wednesday, she _____ sushi at a Japanese restaurant.

4 On Thursday morning, she _____ the bathroom.

5 On Thursday night, she _____ Aziz in hospital.

6 On Friday, she _____ friends to her birthday party.

7 On Saturday, she _____ in the park.

8 On Sunday, she _____ dinner for her parents.

🔊

23.8 LISTEN TO THE AUDIO AND MATCH THE EVENTS TO THE YEARS

Arno describes his life so far.
He mentions important events and
the years in which they happened.

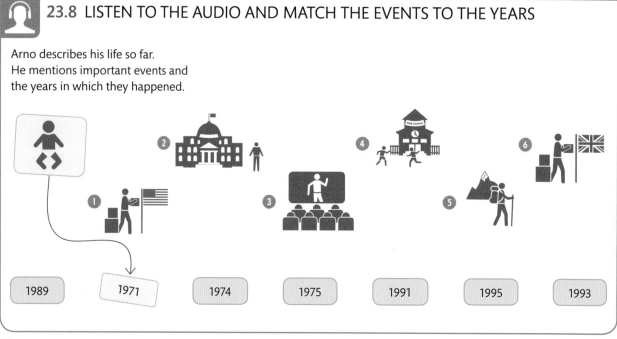

| 1989 | 1971 | 1974 | 1975 | 1991 | 1995 | 1993 |

23.9 KEY LANGUAGE USING "WHEN" WITH THE PAST SIMPLE

To say when in someone's life something happened, you can either use "in" with the year, or "when" with the person's age.

This is the past simple action.

He moved to England in 1990.

He moved to England when he was 10 years old.

This describes when in the past it happened.

🔊

23.10 REWRITE THE SENTENCES ADDING "WHEN" CLAUSES

I started school (four years old). = *I started school when I was four years old.*

① She moved to the US (19 years old). = _____

② They started swimming (25 years old). = _____

③ We visited Japan (27 years old). = _____

④ I received this gift (31 years old). = _____

🔊

23.11 LOOK AT LEONA'S LIFE EVENTS, THEN DESCRIBE EACH ONE OUT LOUD

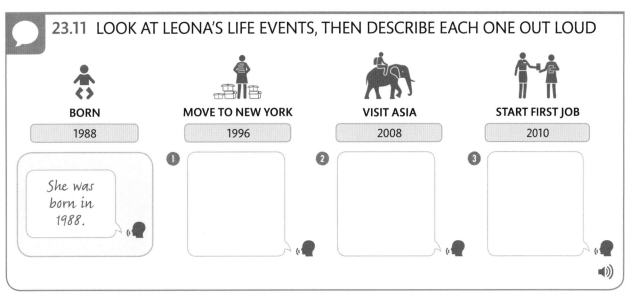

BORN	MOVE TO NEW YORK	VISIT ASIA	START FIRST JOB
1988	1996	2008	2010

She was born in 1988.

① ② ③

🔊

---

24 Past abilities

In the past simple, "can" becomes "could." You often use it to talk about things you "could" do in the past, but can't do now.

⚙ **New language** Using "could" in the past simple
Aa Vocabulary Abilities and pastimes
🧩 **New skill** Talking about past abilities

24.1 KEY LANGUAGE "COULD" FOR PAST ABILITIES

Use "could" to talk about an ability you once had. You can use "when" plus a time setting to say when you had the ability.

Set the time frame with a phrase about an age, day, or year.

 I can't **climb trees now, but I could** when I was younger.

You can use the present simple for contrast.

The statement can be positive using "could" or negative using "couldn't." It doesn't change with the subject.

24.2 FURTHER EXAMPLES "COULD" FOR PAST ABILITIES

When I was a student, I could **study all night before an exam.**

I couldn't **go to China last year because it was too expensive.**

When Milo was eight, he could **play the violin.**

Last year, she couldn't **run very far, but yesterday she ran a marathon.**

24.3 HOW TO FORM "COULD" FOR PAST ABILITIES

"WHEN"	TIME SETTING	"COULD"	ABILITY
When	I was younger,	I could / I couldn't	climb trees.

Begin with "when."

This phrase sets the time in the past when the action was possible.

The statement can be positive or negative.

Use the base form of the verb for the past ability.

24.4 REWRITE THESE SENTENCES IN THE PAST SIMPLE USING "COULD"

I can ski.	I could ski.
① I can cook Italian food.	
② We can't play the piano.	
③ She can paint a picture.	
④ They can't make a cake.	

24.5 LISTEN TO THE AUDIO AND MARK THE CORRECT ANSWERS

When Diana was five, she couldn't...
write music ✓
read music ☐
play the piano. ☐

② When Imelda was seven, she could...
ride a horse ☐
drive a car ☐
fly a plane. ☐

① When Louis was four, he could...
read ☐
write ☐
do mathematics. ☐

③ When Irina was four, she could speak...
one language ☐
two languages ☐
three languages. ☐

24.6 USE THE CHART TO CREATE 16 CORRECT SENTENCES AND SAY THEM OUT LOUD

When I was five, I couldn't play chess.

When I was / When you were	five, seven,	I couldn't / you could	play chess. ride a bike. swim. skate.

Start with a "when" phrase.   Choose an age.   Choose a positive or negative statement.   Finish with an ability.

24 ✔ CHECKLIST

⚙ Using "could" in the past simple ☐   **Aa** Abilities and pastimes ☐   🧩 Talking about past abilities ☐

25.1 ENTERTAINMENT

movie (US)
film (UK)

novel

play

TV show

the news

newspaper

magazine

comedy

science fiction

thriller

documentary

action

horror

musical

romance

crime

hero

villain

audience

clap

movie star

actor

main character

director

author

plot

special effects

stunt

movie theater (US)
cinema (UK)

theater (US)
theatre (UK)

bookstore (US)
bookshop (UK)

exhibition

26 Irregular past verbs

In the past simple, some verbs are irregular. Their past simple forms are not formed using the normal rules, and sometimes look very different from the infinitive forms.

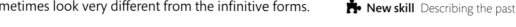

⚙ **New language** Irregular verbs in the past simple
Aa Vocabulary Sequence words
🧩 **New skill** Describing the past

26.1 KEY LANGUAGE IRREGULAR VERBS IN THE PAST SIMPLE

"Go" is the present simple.

I often **go** to the movies.
I **went** last night, but I **didn't go** last week.

"Went" is the past simple of "go."

To make the negative, use "didn't" with the base form.

26.2 HOW TO FORM IRREGULAR VERBS IN THE PAST SIMPLE

Verbs in the past simple do not change with the subject.

This is the past simple of "go."

| SUBJECT | VERB | |
| I | went | to the movies. |

| SUBJECT | NEGATIVE | VERB | |
| I | didn't | go | to the movies. |

Use "did not" or "didn't" to make the negative.

Use the base form of the main verb in the negative.

26.3 FURTHER EXAMPLES IRREGULAR VERBS IN THE PAST SIMPLE

They **had** a great vacation.

He **didn't have** any classes today.

I **came** to the US in 1980.

You **didn't come** to the party.

Aa 26.4 MATCH THE PAST SIMPLE FORMS OF THE VERBS TO THEIR BASE FORMS

put → put

1 began → break
2 broke → take
3 took → sell
4 sold → begin

5 bought → get
6 got → buy
7 wrote → make
8 made → sit
9 sat → write

26.5 READ THE ARTICLE AND NUMBER THE PICTURES IN THE ORDER THEY ARE DESCRIBED

A lucky escape!

A VERY WILD ADVENTURE IN THE FOREST

A few years ago I went camping in Redwood Park with my best friend, Jack. On our first day, we bought some food. We didn't want to stay on the campsite, so instead we walked through the forest to find somewhere else to camp. It got dark early and we were a bit lost so we decided to camp in the middle of the forest. That night, it was really dark and I felt a bit scared, but Jack and I made a fire and sang some songs. It was a quiet night and we slept well.

In the morning, we were hungry so we made our breakfast. But before we ate it, we went to the river. We had a wash and got some fresh water then walked back to our tent. When we got back to the tent, we saw a big brown bear. We didn't move or make a noise. We watched the bear as it sat in our tent and ate all of our breakfast. After that it walked off into the forest with our bags.

Jack and I were very hungry and cold, but we put our tent away and walked away quickly. Then, we ran and ran until finally we found the campsite. We were so happy. It was a very lucky escape!

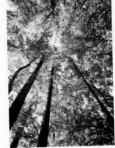

 A ☐
 B ☐
 C 1
 D ☐
 E ☐
 F ☐
 G ☐

26.6 FILL IN THE GAPS IN THIS JOURNAL USING THE WORDS IN THE PANEL

Wow! This morning a bear ___ate___ my breakfast. We are in Redwood Park and last night we camped in the forest. We _____ a fire and it was very quiet, so my friend and I _____ well. The next morning, we _____ to the river to get water. When we got back to the tent, we _____ the bear. I _____ really scared. We _____ back to the campsite and we are safe now!

~~ate~~	slept	made	went	felt	saw	ran

26.7 **VOCABULARY** SEQUENCE WORDS

You use certain words and phrases to help someone understand where you are in the story.

First **he woke up.**   Then **he ate breakfast.**   Next **he had a shower.**   After that **he got dressed.**   Finally **he went to work.**

....

26.8 **FURTHER EXAMPLES** SEQUENCE WORDS

First **I got some money out of the bank.**   Then **I bought some food from the supermarket.**   After that **I had some coffee.**

In the morning **we watched the sun rise over the Serengeti.**   Then **we saw the birds fly off.**   Finally **the lions appeared.**

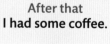

26.9 REWRITE THE SENTENCES PUTTING THE SEQUENCE WORDS IN THE CORRECT PLACES

I won the game. I got a prize. **(then)**
I won the game. Then I got a prize.

3 Ben passed his test. He bought a car. **(next)**
_____

1 Sheila put her best clothes on. **(first)**
_____

4 Eat dinner. You can have some dessert. **(after that)**
_____

2 Do your homework. Go out and play. **(first, then)**
_____

5 He ate a large breakfast. **(first)**
_____

26.10 FILL IN THE GAPS USING SEQUENCE WORDS, THEN SAY THE STORY OUT LOUD

____First____ Harold and Jack bought some food. ____Then____ they went to the forest.

1 _____ they got lost. Then they decided to camp and put the tent up.

2 They were scared of the sounds in the forest. But _____ they went to sleep.

3 _____ they washed in the river. They went back to their tent for food.

4 _____ they saw a bear eating their food. After that, it walked into the forest.

5 _____ Harold and Jack arrived safely back at the campsite.

~~first~~	after that	~~then~~	finally
finally	after that	in the morning	

89

26.11 KEY LANGUAGE IRREGULAR VERBS, QUESTIONS IN THE PAST SIMPLE

Use the past simple of "do" plus
the base verb form to ask a question.

In the statement the main
verb is in the past simple.

They bought a new car.   **She saw the show last night.**

Did they buy a new car?   **Did she see the show last night?**

"Did" is in the
past simple of "do."

The main verb
is in its base form.

26.12 FURTHER EXAMPLES IRREGULAR VERBS, QUESTIONS IN THE PAST SIMPLE

Did they have a good time?   **Did she meet her friends in town?**

Did you read a book on the beach?   **Did he go to the gym?**

Aa 26.13 MATCH THE QUESTIONS AND ANSWERS

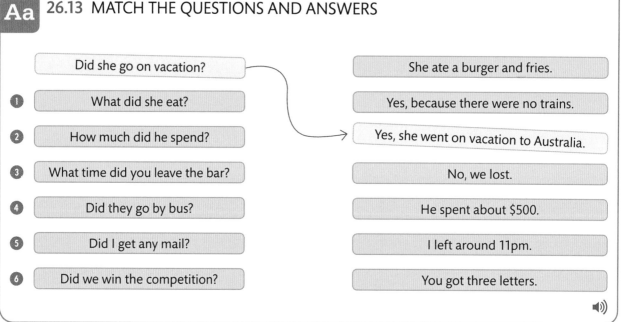

Question	Answer
Did she go on vacation?	She ate a burger and fries.
❶ What did she eat?	Yes, because there were no trains.
❷ How much did he spend?	Yes, she went on vacation to Australia.
❸ What time did you leave the bar?	No, we lost.
❹ Did they go by bus?	He spent about $500.
❺ Did I get any mail?	I left around 11pm.
❻ Did we win the competition?	You got three letters.

26.14 FILL IN THE GAPS TO WRITE QUESTIONS BASED ON THE SENTENCES

They sold 50 cakes.

How many _cakes did they sell?_

1 The movie began at 7:30pm.

When _____

2 He chose the red shirt.

Which_____

3 She ate pasta last night.

What _____

4 She read the magazine this morning.

What _____

5 Aia caught five fish at the lake.

How many _____

6 You saw Michelle at the party last night.

Who _____

7 He gave his brother a new sweater.

What _____

◀))

26.15 LISTEN TO THE AUDIO AND ANSWER THE QUESTIONS

Daniella and Marcus are talking about their friend's birthday party.

When did Daniella arrive at the party?
7pm ☐
8pm ☑
9pm ☐

1 What did she wear?
a red dress ☐
a green skirt ☐
her jeans ☐

2 What gift did she give her friend?
a watch ☐
flowers ☐
a book ☐

3 Who did she meet at the party?
Sam ☐
Lana ☐
Will ☐

4 What did she eat at the party?
burger ☐
pizza ☐
chicken ☐

5 Which music did she dance to?
jazz ☐
rock ☐
pop ☐

26 ✓ CHECKLIST

⚙️ Irregular verbs in the past simple ☐   Aa Sequence words ☐   🧩 Describing the past ☐

27.1 TOOLS

| tape measure | hammer | clamp | file | hacksaw |

| screwdriver | nut | bolt | screw | nail |

| pliers | wrench (US)
spanner (UK) | | | |

| trowel | shears | fork | spade | hoe | rake |

saw

drill

jigsaw

level (US)
spirit level (UK)

27.2 KITCHEN IMPLEMENTS

grater

peeler

whisk

cutting board (US)
chopping board (UK)

kitchen knife

scissors

can opener (US)
tin opener (UK)

bottle opener

corkscrew

wooden spoon

spatula

ladle

28 Telling a story

You can use "about" to describe the subject matter of movies, shows, and stories. Use adjectives to make a description more specific.

⚙ **New language** "About," opinions
Aa Vocabulary Opinions
🧩 **New skill** Describing media and culture

28.1 KEY LANGUAGE USING "ABOUT" TO DESCRIBE MEDIA AND CULTURE

Use "about" to give more information about a movie, play, show, story, or book.

It's a movie
It's a story
The play is

about

a mystery.
a lawyer.
two brothers.

This introduces what the subject matter of the story is.

This is the additional information on the story.

28.2 FURTHER EXAMPLES USING "ABOUT" TO DESCRIBE MEDIA AND CULTURE

The movie is a thriller about two New York police officers.

It's a story about a young couple in the countryside.

The book is about a French city during the 1920s.

28.3 LISTEN TO THE AUDIO AND NUMBER THE MOVIES IN THE ORDER THEY ARE DESCRIBED

A ☐   B ☐   C 1   D ☐   E ☐

28.4 KEY LANGUAGE DESCRIBING YOUR OPINIONS

You can use verbs in the past simple to give your opinions. Use "because" plus adjectives to give your reasons.

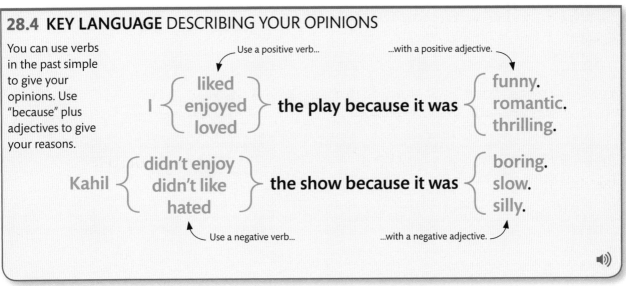

Use a positive verb...

I { liked / enjoyed / loved } the play because it was { funny. / romantic. / thrilling. }

...with a positive adjective.

Kahil { didn't enjoy / didn't like / hated } the show because it was { boring. / slow. / silly. }

Use a negative verb...   ...with a negative adjective.

28.5 LISTEN TO THE AUDIO AND ANSWER THE QUESTIONS

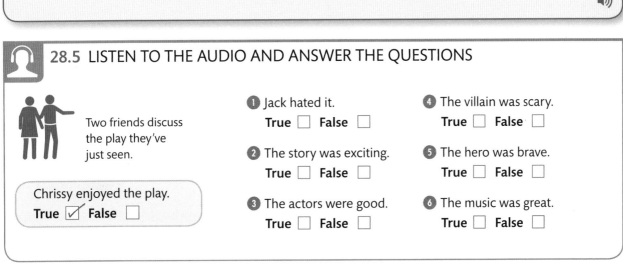

Two friends discuss the play they've just seen.

Chrissy enjoyed the play.
True ☑ **False** ☐

1 Jack hated it.
True ☐ **False** ☐

2 The story was exciting.
True ☐ **False** ☐

3 The actors were good.
True ☐ **False** ☐

4 The villain was scary.
True ☐ **False** ☐

5 The hero was brave.
True ☐ **False** ☐

6 The music was great.
True ☐ **False** ☐

28.6 USE THE CHART TO CREATE 12 CORRECT SENTENCES AND SAY THEM OUT LOUD

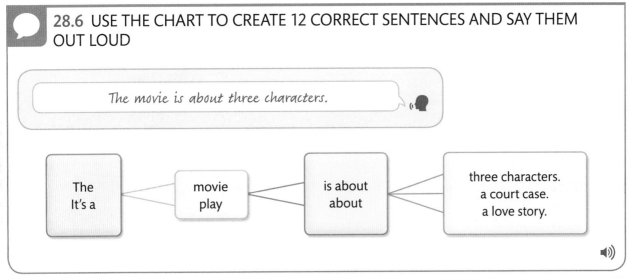

The movie is about three characters.

| The / It's a | movie / play | is about / about | three characters. / a court case. / a love story. |

28.7 READ THE REVIEW AND ANSWER THE QUESTIONS

Millie's Magic!
The latest show in town is a hit

Millie's Magical Music is a wonderful new show. The story is about a little girl called Millie. She loves singing. In her bedroom, she listens to songs and learns how to sing them. At school, she has a kind English teacher called Miss Graham and a terrible music teacher called Miss Cafferty, who is the villain of the story. Both Miss Graham and Miss Cafferty hear Millie's beautiful voice. Miss Graham wants everyone to hear Millie, but Miss Cafferty wants to stop her singing.

It's an enjoyable story about music, friendship, and hope.

Many of the actors in this musical are children and they are all excellent, especially Millie. The songs in the musical are very good, too.

I really liked the music. It's a hit!

> What type of show is it?
> _It is a musical._

1 What does Millie enjoy?

_____

2 Where does she learn to sing?

_____

3 What is the name of her music teacher?

_____

4 Who is the villain?

_____

5 Is Millie played by an adult?

_____

28.8 REWRITE THESE SENTENCES USING NEGATIVE WORDS

> The musical was wonderful.
> _The musical was awful._

1 Millie loves singing.

_____

2 Millie has beautiful costumes.

_____

3 Many of the actors were excellent.

_____

4 The songs are very good.

_____

5 I really loved the music.

_____

| bad | hated | ~~awful~~ | hates | terrible | ugly |

Aa 28.9 READ THE CLUES AND WRITE THE ANSWERS IN THE GRID

1 The bad guy, the hero fights this person

2 A true story with real people, not actors

3 A funny story that makes people laugh

4 A story told in a theater

5 A person who writes novels

6 An exciting story

adventure   author   play

comedy   ~~villain~~   documentary

1 v i l l a i n

---

28 ✓ CHECKLIST

⚙ "About," opinions ☐   Aa Opinions ☐   🧩 Describing media and culture ☐

↻ REVIEW THE ENGLISH YOU HAVE LEARNED IN UNITS 21–28

NEW LANGUAGE	SAMPLE SENTENCE	☑	UNIT
WRITING AND SAYING DATES	His birthday is on May 10. My meeting is on the 18th of May.	☐	21.1, 21.2
"TO BE" STATEMENTS AND QUESTIONS ABOUT THE PAST	She was a student in 1985. Was he in India last year? He wasn't in France.	☐	22.1, 22.7
REGULAR VERBS IN THE PAST SIMPLE	I visited Luke last Friday. I didn't play tennis.	☐	23.1
USING "COULD" FOR PAST ABILITIES	I could climb trees when I was younger.	☐	24.1
IRREGULAR VERBS IN THE PAST SIMPLE	I went to the movies last night. I didn't go last week.	☐	26.1
GIVING OPINIONS ABOUT CULTURE	It's a movie about two brothers. I enjoyed it because it was thrilling.	☐	28.1, 28.4

29 Asking about the past

You can make questions in the past simple using "did." This is useful for asking about past events, such as travel and vacations.

🔧 **New language** Past simple questions
Aa Vocabulary Travel and activities
🧩 **New skill** Talking about vacations

29.1 KEY LANGUAGE "YES / NO" QUESTIONS IN THE PAST SIMPLE

Use the auxiliary verb "did" to make questions in the past simple that have "yes/no" answers.

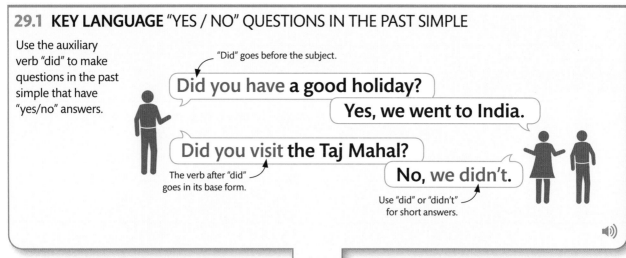

"Did" goes before the subject.

Did you have a good holiday?

Yes, we went to India.

Did you visit the Taj Mahal?

The verb after "did" goes in its base form.

No, we didn't.

Use "did" or "didn't" for short answers.

29.2 FURTHER EXAMPLES "YES / NO" QUESTIONS IN THE PAST SIMPLE

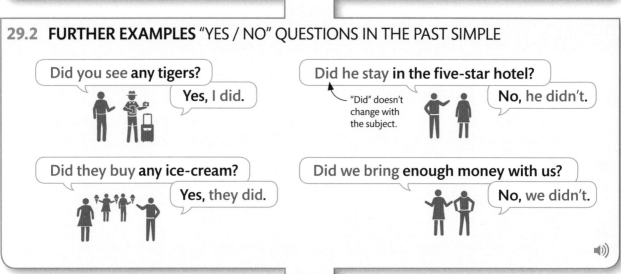

Did you see any tigers?

Yes, I did.

Did he stay in the five-star hotel?

"Did" doesn't change with the subject.

No, he didn't.

Did they buy any ice-cream?

Yes, they did.

Did we bring enough money with us?

No, we didn't.

29.3 HOW IT IS FORMED "YES / NO" QUESTIONS IN THE PAST SIMPLE

"DID"	SUBJECT	VERB	OBJECT
Did	you	visit	the Taj Mahal?

29.4 LISTEN TO THE AUDIO, THEN NUMBER THE PICTURES IN THE ORDER THEY ARE DESCRIBED

Bea talks about her vacation in India.

A

B 1

C

D

E

29.5 MATCH THE QUESTIONS TO THE SHORT ANSWERS

Did you get the job?

Yes, we did.

1 Did I have lunch today?

Yes, I did.

2 Did the dog eat its dinner?

No, you didn't.

3 Did they go to Venezuela?

Yes, it did.

4 Did we win the competition?

No, they didn't.

🔊

29.6 REWRITE THE SENTENCES AS QUESTIONS

They went paragliding in Greece.
Did they go paragliding in Greece?

1 They gave Ellie a present.
_____

2 You stayed in an expensive hotel.
_____

3 His mother bought a lot of postcards.
_____

4 Your brother climbed a mountain.
_____

5 Their parents took lots of photos.
_____

🔊

29.7 KEY LANGUAGE QUESTION WORDS WITH THE PAST SIMPLE

The question word goes at the beginning of the question, followed by "did" and the subject.

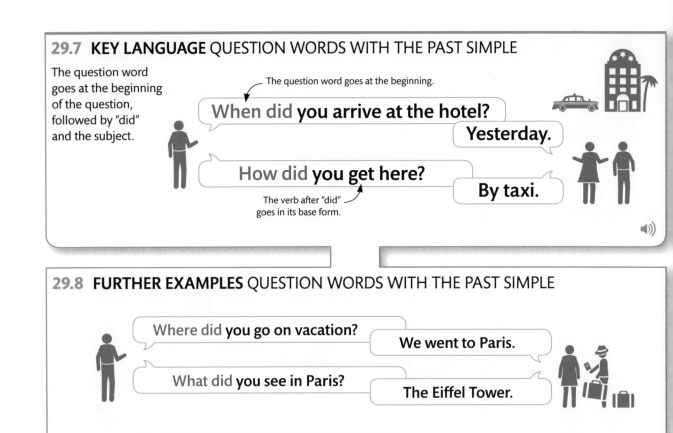

The question word goes at the beginning.

When did you arrive at the hotel?

Yesterday.

How did you get here?

By taxi.

The verb after "did" goes in its base form.

29.8 FURTHER EXAMPLES QUESTION WORDS WITH THE PAST SIMPLE

Where did you go on vacation?

We went to Paris.

What did you see in Paris?

The Eiffel Tower.

What did you do on vacation?

We went hiking.

When did you come home?

This morning.

29.9 MATCH THE QUESTIONS WITH THE CORRECT ANSWERS

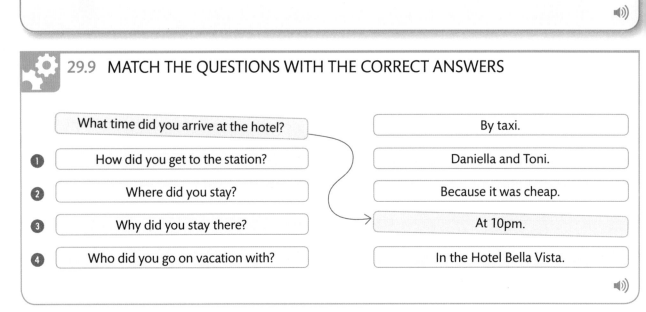

What time did you arrive at the hotel? — At 10pm.

By taxi.

1. How did you get to the station?

Daniella and Toni.

2. Where did you stay?

Because it was cheap.

3. Why did you stay there?

At 10pm.

4. Who did you go on vacation with?

In the Hotel Bella Vista.

29.10 READ THE EMAIL AND ANSWER THE QUESTIONS

To: Sam

Subject: Trip to New York

Hi Sam,

We're having a great time in New York. There's so much to do. We arrived on Friday and went up the Empire State Building. Then, on Saturday, we took the boat to Staten Island and saw the Statue of Liberty. I was surprised because it looked quite small. Yesterday, I went to a store called Macy's and bought some nice clothes. Then we went to a famous restaurant in Grand Central Station and ate oysters.

Love from Sue xx

When did she arrive in New York?
On Monday ☐ **On Thursday** ☐ **On Friday** ☑

1 How did she get to Staten Island?
By taxi ☐ **By boat** ☐ **By bus** ☐

2 When did she see the Statue of Liberty?
On Friday ☐ **On Saturday** ☐ **Yesterday** ☐

3 Which store did she go to?
Macy's ☐ **Bloomingdale's** ☐ **Saks Fifth Avenue** ☐

4 What did she buy there?
Some shoes ☐ **Some perfume** ☐ **Some clothes** ☐

5 What did Sue eat in Grand Central Station?
A hamburger ☐ **Oysters** ☐ **Steak and salad** ☐

29.11 SAY THE QUESTIONS OUT LOUD, FILLING IN THE GAPS

When _did you visit China_ ?
We visited China in 2011.

1 Who _____ ?
I went on vacation with Jo.

2 Where _____ ?
We stayed in a hotel in London.

3 What _____ ?
We ate fried rice in Chinatown.

4 How _____ for?
We went abroad for six months.

5 When _____ ?
We left the US on June 29th.

---

29 ✓ CHECKLIST

⚙ Past simple questions ☐   **Aa** Travel and activities ☐   🧩 Talking about vacations ☐

30 Applying for a job

If you want to find a job, you need to understand the English words and phrases used in advertisements and on recruitment websites.

⚙️ **New language** Interview responses
Aa Vocabulary Job words and phrases
🧩 **New skill** Dealing with job applications

30.1 VOCABULARY APPLYING FOR A JOB

look for a job

**résumé (US)
curriculum vitae / CV (UK)**

apply for a job

have an interview

get the job

start the job

🔊

30.2 READ THE JOB ADVERTISEMENTS AND ANSWER THE QUESTIONS

26 BUSINESS TODAY

JOBS

WANTED: Assistant chef at Marie's Cakes, Ohio. Can you cook? Do you love cake? We need an assistant chef on Saturdays and Sundays (6am to 2pm), $10 per hour.

WANTED: Teacher at summer school, Alaska. Do you like children? You can teach kids aged 11 to 14 this summer (June to August). Some experience needed.

WANTED: Gardener at St. Bernard's College, Idaho. We need a gardener to work part-time in our beautiful gardens. Experience needed. 20 hours per week.

The job at Marie's Cakes is for Fridays and Saturdays.
True ☐ **False** ☑

1 The job at Marie's Cakes is in Ohio.
True ☐ **False** ☐

2 The teaching job starts in August.
True ☐ **False** ☐

3 You will teach children aged 11 to 14 years old.
True ☐ **False** ☐

4 The gardening job is full-time.
True ☐ **False** ☐

5 The gardening job is at a castle.
True ☐ **False** ☐

30.3 VOCABULARY WORDS IN YOUR RÉSUMÉ

qualification ....

work experience ....

hobby ....

interest ....

reference ....

Aa 30.4 FILL IN THE GAPS USING THE WORDS IN THE PANEL

I need to give the interviewer a _____reference_____ from my last boss.

1 My _____ include degrees in biology and chemistry.

2 The interview at the bank went really well. I've _____ .

3 The manager read my _____ and said it was really good.

4 I can _____ the job in January.

5 You need to _____ before you can get the job.

| have an interview | reference | qualifications | résumé | got the job | start |

30.5 LISTEN TO THE AUDIO, THEN NUMBER THE QUESTIONS IN THE ORDER THAT YOU HEAR THEM

Tom Willis is being interviewed for a job.

Ⓐ Why do you want this job? ☐

Ⓑ What did you do at the store? ☐

Ⓒ Why did you study English at college? 1

Ⓓ When can you start work? ☐

Ⓔ Why did you leave the music store? ☐

Ⓕ Are you good at working with people? ☐

30 ✓ CHECKLIST

⚙ Interview responses ☐   **Aa** Job words and phrases ☐   🧩 Dealing with job applications ☐

31 Types of questions

There are two kinds of question: subject questions and object questions. You form them in different ways in order to ask about different things.

⚙ **New language** Subject and object questions
Aa Vocabulary Workplace words
🧩 **New skill** Asking different kinds of question

31.1 KEY LANGUAGE OBJECT QUESTIONS

Use object questions to ask who received an action, not who did the action. They are called object questions because the question word is the object of the main verb.

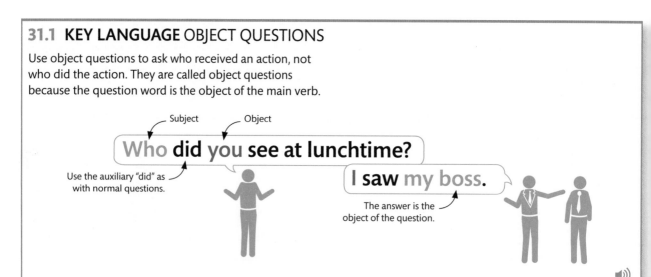

Subject
Object

Who did you see at lunchtime?

Use the auxiliary "did" as with normal questions.

I saw my boss.

The answer is the object of the question.

31.2 FURTHER EXAMPLES OBJECT QUESTIONS

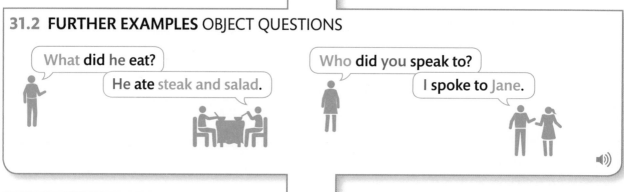

What **did he eat?**

He **ate** steak and salad.

Who **did you speak to?**

I **spoke to** Jane.

31.3 HOW TO FORM OBJECT QUESTIONS

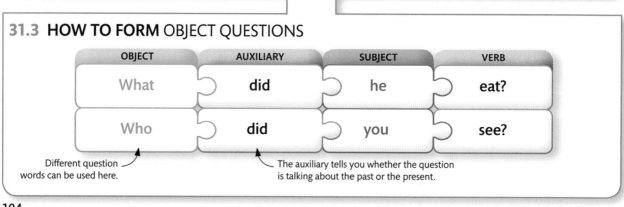

OBJECT	AUXILIARY	SUBJECT	VERB
What	did	he	eat?
Who	did	you	see?

Different question words can be used here.

The auxiliary tells you whether the question is talking about the past or the present.

31.4 VOCABULARY IN THE WORKPLACE

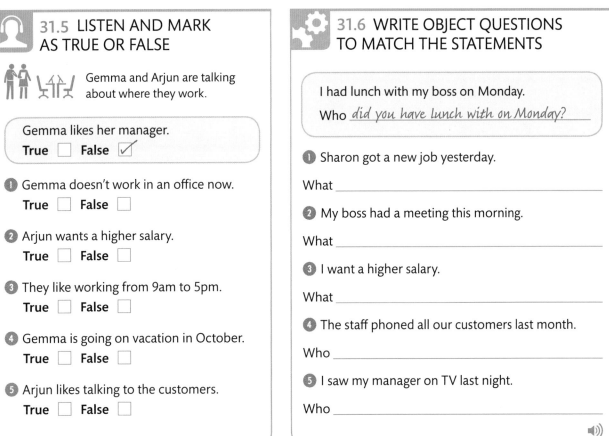

customer

boss

manager

salary

pay

staff

company

nine-to-five job

part-time

full-time

31.5 LISTEN AND MARK AS TRUE OR FALSE

Gemma and Arjun are talking about where they work.

Gemma likes her manager.
True ☐ **False** ☑

1 Gemma doesn't work in an office now.
True ☐ **False** ☐

2 Arjun wants a higher salary.
True ☐ **False** ☐

3 They like working from 9am to 5pm.
True ☐ **False** ☐

4 Gemma is going on vacation in October.
True ☐ **False** ☐

5 Arjun likes talking to the customers.
True ☐ **False** ☐

31.6 WRITE OBJECT QUESTIONS TO MATCH THE STATEMENTS

I had lunch with my boss on Monday.
Who _did you have lunch with on Monday?_

1 Sharon got a new job yesterday.
What _____

2 My boss had a meeting this morning.
What _____

3 I want a higher salary.
What _____

4 The staff phoned all our customers last month.
Who _____

5 I saw my manager on TV last night.
Who _____

31.7 KEY LANGUAGE SUBJECT QUESTIONS

Use subject questions to ask who did the action. They are called subject questions because the question word is the subject of the main verb.

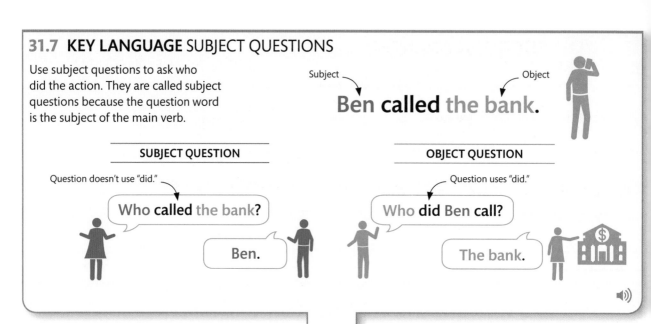

Subject → Ben **called** the bank. ← Object

SUBJECT QUESTION

Question doesn't use "did." →

Who **called** the bank?

Ben.

OBJECT QUESTION

Question uses "did." →

Who **did** Ben **call?**

The bank.

31.8 FURTHER EXAMPLES SUBJECT AND OBJECT QUESTIONS

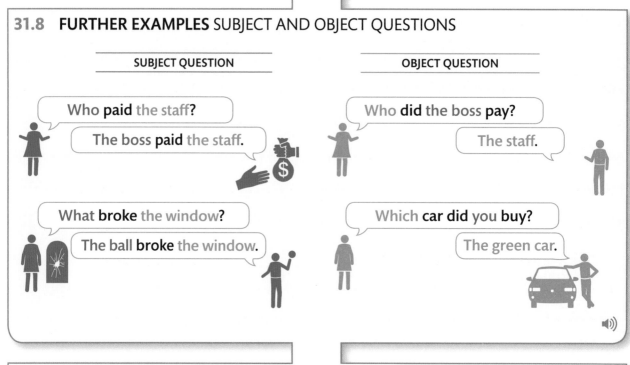

SUBJECT QUESTION

Who **paid** the staff?

The boss **paid** the staff.

What **broke** the window?

The ball **broke** the window.

OBJECT QUESTION

Who **did** the boss **pay?**

The staff.

Which **car did** you **buy?**

The green car.

31.9 HOW TO FORM SUBJECT QUESTIONS

"Who" is the most common pronoun used in subject questions, but you might hear others.

SUBJECT	VERB	OBJECT
Who	called	the bank?

31.10 PUT THE WORDS IN THE CORRECT ORDER

this letter | sent | last week? | Who

Who sent this letter last week?

1 did | manager | say? | the | What

_____

2 speak to? | customer | Which | you | did

_____

3 Emma | book? | gave | Who | that

_____

4 7am? | What | at | started

_____

🔊

31.11 MARK THE CORRECT VERSION OF THE QUESTION

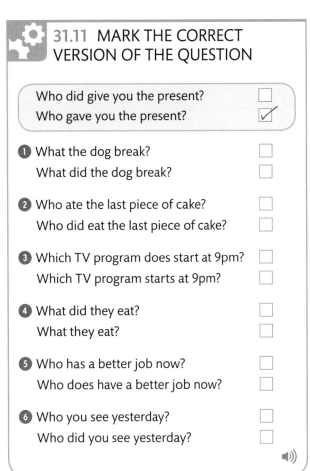

Who did give you the present? ☐
Who gave you the present? ☑

1 What the dog break? ☐
What did the dog break? ☐

2 Who ate the last piece of cake? ☐
Who did eat the last piece of cake? ☐

3 Which TV program does start at 9pm? ☐
Which TV program starts at 9pm? ☐

4 What did they eat? ☐
What they eat? ☐

5 Who has a better job now? ☐
Who does have a better job now? ☐

6 Who you see yesterday? ☐
Who did you see yesterday? ☐

🔊

31.12 WRITE QUESTIONS TO MATCH THE STATEMENTS

His old manager paid him a higher salary.
Who _paid him a higher salary?_

1 Arjun started a full-time job last month.

What _____

2 The office has a new door.

What _____

3 The customers are waiting outside.

Who _____

4 Mark wants to be a teacher.

What _____

5 The boss wants a new office this year.

What _____

🔊

31 ✓ CHECKLIST

⚙ Subject and object questions ☐   **Aa** Workplace words ☐   🧩 Asking different kinds of question ☐

32 Someone, anyone, everyone

Use indefinite pronouns, such as "anyone," "someone,"
and "everyone," to refer to a person or a group of people
without explaining who they are.

⚙ **New language** Indefinite pronouns
Aa Vocabulary Office words
🧩 **New skill** Talking about people in general

32.1 KEY LANGUAGE "ANYONE / SOMEONE"

Use "someone" or
"somebody" to refer
to a person in a
positive statement,
and "anyone" or
"anybody" for a
question or a
negative statement.

You can also use "anybody."
Both words mean: any person.

Did anyone call me this morning?

Yes, someone called you at 11 o'clock.

You can also use "somebody."
Both words mean: a person.

32.2 FURTHER EXAMPLES "ANYONE / SOMEONE"

Someone is working late.

Did anyone buy a gift for Mrs. Tan?

Somebody left this letter on my desk.

I didn't give anybody your name.

The statement is negative,
so use "anybody/anyone."

32.3 CROSS OUT THE INCORRECT WORD IN EACH SENTENCE

I saw ~~anyone~~ / someone at reception this morning.

1 Please ask anyone / someone to phone Mr. Richards immediately.

2 Mrs. Turner didn't give anyone / someone any work to do this week.

3 Can I give anyone / someone a lift to the station tomorrow morning?

4 Mr. Phillips needs anyone / someone to go with him to the hospital.

5 I'm sorry, but there isn't anyone / someone in the office at the moment.

32.4 KEY LANGUAGE "EVERYONE / NO ONE"

Use "everyone" or "everybody" to refer to the whole group in a statement or question. "No one" or "nobody" means none of the group.

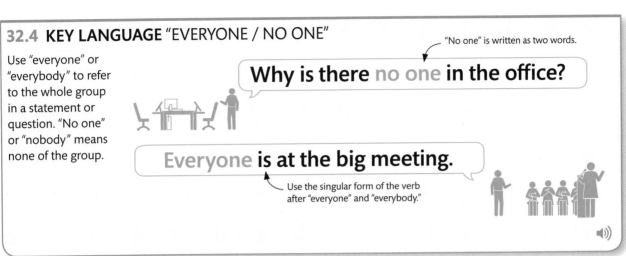

"No one" is written as two words.

Why is there no one in the office?

Everyone is at the big meeting.

Use the singular form of the verb after "everyone" and "everybody."

32.5 LISTEN TO THE AUDIO AND CROSS OUT THE INCORRECT WORD IN EACH SENTENCE

~~Everybody~~ / Somebody wants to have a meeting this afternoon.

1. Nobody / Somebody in room 212 needs a new computer.

2. Theodore tells everyone / someone the good news about the business.

3. Everyone / Anybody is going for lunch at the restaurant to celebrate Daniella's birthday.

4. Nobody / Somebody closed the window last night before they left the office.

5. Everyone / Anyone knows that we have a new office.

32.6 USE THE CHART TO CREATE 12 CORRECT SENTENCES AND SAY THEM OUT LOUD

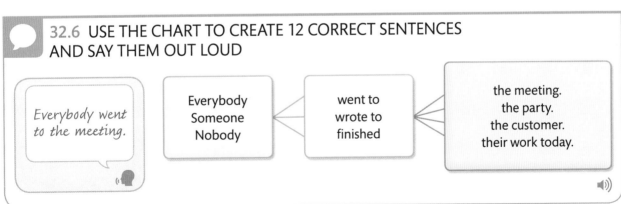

Everybody went to the meeting.

Everybody	went to	the meeting.
Someone	wrote to	the party.
Nobody	finished	the customer.
		their work today.

32 ✓ CHECKLIST

⚙ Indefinite pronouns ☐   **Aa** Office words ☐   🧩 Talking about people in general ☐

33 Making conversation

Short questions are a way of showing interest when you are talking with someone. Use them to keep the conversation going.

🔧 **New language** Short questions
Aa Vocabulary Question words
🧩 **New skill** Asking short questions

33.1 KEY LANGUAGE SHORT QUESTIONS

You already know the answers to short questions. Use them to invite the person speaking to say more.

For many verbs, use the auxiliary verb "do" to form the question.

I went **to the movies last night.**

Did you?

Yes, I saw that new thriller. It was **really exciting.**

Was it?

With the verb "to be," invert the word order in the statement to make the short question.

33.2 FURTHER EXAMPLES SHORT QUESTIONS

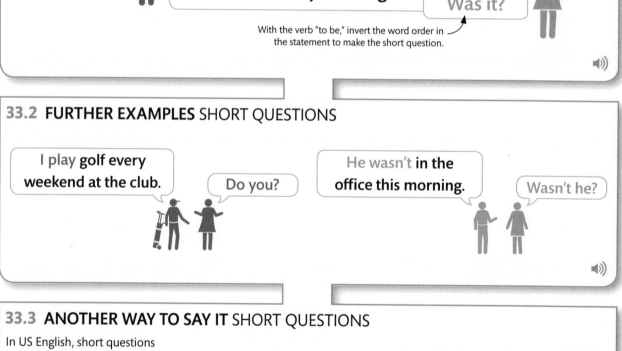

I play **golf every weekend at the club.**

Do you?

He wasn't **in the office this morning.**

Wasn't he?

33.3 ANOTHER WAY TO SAY IT SHORT QUESTIONS

In US English, short questions are sometimes not inverted.

They didn't go **to the theater last night.**

They didn't?

There isn't **any milk left in the fridge.**

There isn't?

33.4 MATCH THE STATEMENTS TO THE SHORT QUESTIONS

Laura went paragliding. → She did?

Didn't you?

1 I was very tired last night.

2 We didn't go to the party.

Does it?

3 Frank wasn't feeling well.

Were you?

4 The cat likes its new food.

He wasn't?

33.5 COMPLETE THE SHORT QUESTIONS, SPEAKING OUT LOUD

Frank really likes jazz.

_____ *Does* _____ he?

1 It was very hot in Spain.

_____ it?

2 There is a cup of coffee for you here.

There _____ ?

3 I gave the money to Mr. Singh last night.

_____ you?

---

33 ✓ CHECKLIST

⚙ Short questions ☐   **Aa** Question words ☐   🧩 Asking short questions ☐

♻ REVIEW THE ENGLISH YOU HAVE LEARNED IN UNITS 29-33

NEW LANGUAGE	SAMPLE SENTENCE	☑	UNIT
QUESTIONS IN THE PAST SIMPLE	"Did you have a good vacation?" "Yes, we went to India."	☐	29.1, 29.3, 29.7
SUBJECT AND OBJECT QUESTIONS	Who did you see at lunchtime? Who did Ben call?	☐	31.1, 31.7, 31.8
"SOMEONE" AND "ANYONE"	"Did anyone call me this morning?" "Yes, someone called at 11 o'clock."	☐	32.1, 32.2
"EVERYONE" AND "NO ONE"	"Why is there no one in the office?" "Everyone is at the big meeting."	☐	32.4
SHORT QUESTIONS	"I went to the movies last night." "Did you?" "It was really exciting." "Was it?"	☐	33.1, 33.2

34.1 GOING OUT

art gallery

book club

night club

concert hall

fun fair

circus

restaurant

bar

menu

waiter

waitress

check (US)
bill (UK)

ballet

opera

band

orchestra

musician

festival

concert

show

audience

applause

meet friends

go clubbing

go dancing

go to a party

go to a restaurant

go to the movies (US)
go to the cinema (UK)

see a play

do karaoke

go bowling

buy a ticket

35 Future arrangements

You can use the present continuous to talk about things that are happening now. You can also use it to talk about arrangements for the future.

⚙ **New language** Future with present continuous
Aa Vocabulary Excuses
🧩 **New skill** Talking about future arrangements

35.1 KEY LANGUAGE PRESENT CONTINUOUS WITH FUTURE EVENTS

Use time phrases to show whether a verb in the present continuous refers to the present or the future.

"At the moment" refers to the present.

Present continuous refers to Dave's present activity.

At the moment Dave is working, but tomorrow he is playing golf.

Time clause "tomorrow" refers to the future.

Present continuous refers to a future event that is planned.

35.2 FURTHER EXAMPLES PRESENT CONTINUOUS WITH FUTURE EVENTS

Jack's playing **soccer** now, **then** later he's seeing **a movie**.

Sue is studying now, **but** this evening she's visiting **a friend**.

Today, I'm playing **tennis, but** I'm playing **golf** tomorrow.

You can use the time word or phrase at the start or end of a clause.

I'm reading at the moment, **but** I'm going **running** later.

35.3 KEY LANGUAGE "ON / IN" WITH DAYS, MONTHS, AND DATES

Use the preposition "on" in front of days of the week and specific dates. Use "in" with months and years.

I'm working on Tuesday.

I'm working on May 9th.

I'm retiring in June.

I'm retiring in 2035.

35.4 FILL IN THE GAPS BY PUTTING THE VERBS IN THE PRESENT CONTINUOUS

I _____ *am watching* _____ (watch 👫) TV with my friends tonight.

1 John's cousins _____ (come 🎉) to the party tomorrow.

2 I _____ (go 💆) to the dentist tomorrow morning.

3 My family and I _____ (visit 🚪) my grandma on Saturday.

4 The managers in my office _____ (have 🪑) a meeting this afternoon.

5 A famous band _____ (play 🎸) in Central Park this weekend.

6 He _____ (study 📚) for his exam tomorrow.

🔊

35.5 LISTEN TO THE AUDIO, THEN NUMBER THE PICTURES IN THE ORDER YOU HEAR THEM

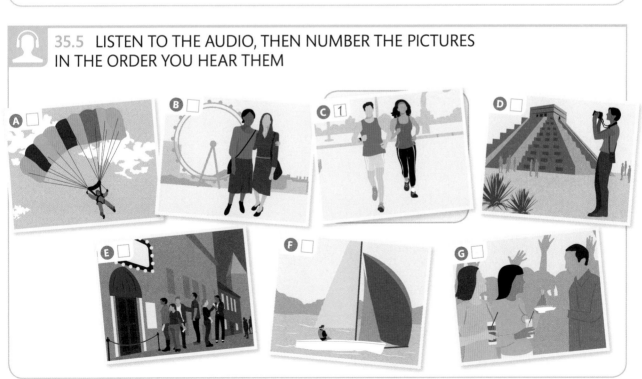

A ☐   B ☐   C 1   D ☐

E ☐   F ☐   G ☐

35.6 KEY LANGUAGE MAKING EXCUSES

Sometimes you need to say why you can't do something. To be polite, use an expression like "Sorry, I can't" before saying what your other plans are.

Would you like to go to the movies tonight?

Sorry, I can't. I'm working late.

To be polite, apologize first.

Use the present continuous to say what you are doing instead.

35.7 FURTHER EXAMPLES MAKING EXCUSES

I'd like to, but I'm going **to the dentist.**

I'd love to, but I'm meeting **friends.**

That would be fun, but I'm visiting **family.**

That sounds nice, but I'm playing **baseball.**

35.8 REWRITE THE SENTENCES, PUTTING THE WORDS IN THE CORRECT ORDER

| tonight. | fun, but | theater | That | the | I'm | going to | would be |

That would be fun, but I'm going to the theater tonight.

❶ | my | parents | I'm | Sorry, I can't. | visiting | this | evening. |

❷ | this | like to, | but | weekend. | I'd | France | going to | I'm |

❸ | sounds | but | I'm going | That | on Tuesday. | nice, | swimming |

❹ | love to, | I'm | looking after | I'd | my nephew | tomorrow. | but |

116

35.9 ANSWER EACH INVITATION OUT LOUD, USING AN EXCUSE FROM THE DIARY

September 2020

21 SATURDAY

9am – Play soccer with Eva.

Noon – Go to lunch with Aziz.

1:30–3pm – Look after Sandy's baby.

4pm – Go to yoga class.

6pm – Go to dinner with Marco and Olivia.

7:30pm – Go to the theater to see a musical.

Would you like to come swimming at 9am?

I'd love to, but _I'm playing soccer with Eva._

1 Would you like to come to dinner tonight?

I'd like to, but _____

2 Would you like to go to lunch today?

Sorry, I can't. _____

3 Would you like to play tennis at 7:30pm?

That would be fun, but _____

4 Would you like to go shopping at 2pm?

That sounds nice, but _____

5 Would you like to go to a dance class at 4pm?

I'd like to, but _____

---

35 ✓ CHECKLIST

⚙ Future with present continuous ☐   **Aa** Excuses ☐   🧩 Talking about future arrangements ☐

36 Plans and intentions

You can use "going to" to talk about what you want to do in the future. Use it also to talk about specific plans, such as when and where you're going to do something.

⚙ **New language** Future tense
Aa Vocabulary Time words and phrases
🧩 **New skill** Talking about your plans

36.1 KEY LANGUAGE "GOING TO" FOR FUTURE PLANS

Use the verb "to be" with "going to" to say what you plan to do.

Base form of verb.

I'm going to **buy a new car.**

We are going to **cook dinner tonight.**

"Going to" doesn't change with the subject.

Use a time word or time phrase to say when you will cook dinner.

🔊

36.2 FURTHER EXAMPLES "GOING TO" FOR FUTURE PLANS

I'm going to **start this book soon.**

Sam's going to **get fit before his next birthday.**

We're going to **cycle from Boston to Cape Cod next weekend.**

I'm not going to **eat any chocolate this month.**

Add "not" after the verb "to be" to make the negative.

🔊

36.3 HOW TO FORM "GOING TO" FOR FUTURE PLANS

SUBJECT	"TO BE"	"GOING TO"	BASE FORM OF VERB	REST OF SENTENCE
He	is	going to	buy	a new car.

36.4 FILL IN THE GAPS PUTTING THE VERBS IN THE FUTURE WITH "GOING TO"

Darren and Miki _____*are going to watch*_____ (watch) a movie tonight.

1 I _____ (not eat) sushi for dinner.

2 Debra _____ (get) a new job soon.

3 My friends _____ (cook) a meal for me next week.

4 Manuel _____ (learn) how to scuba dive this summer.

5 We _____ (travel) to Dubai in December.

36.5 READ THE ARTICLE AND ANSWER THE QUESTIONS

14   The Weekly You

WHAT ARE YOUR RESOLUTIONS?

Exercise more or stop eating chocolate? It's a question many of us ask ourselves as the year ends.

Betty from California makes one resolution every year. "I'm not going to give up smoking," she tells us, "because I did that last time. This year, I'm going to get fit!"

In the US only 8 percent of people keep to their resolutions. Many give up by the end of January.

A lot of people make resolutions, but Australian Joanna Gee makes one resolution for every day of the year. That's 365 resolutions every year.

"I love making resolutions," Joanna says. "This year I'm going to do more unusual things. On June 23 I'm going to climb a mountain, and then on September 30 I'm going to swim with sharks."

Betty has one resolution this year.
True ☑ **False** ☐

1 Betty is going to give up smoking this year.
True ☐ **False** ☐

2 Only 8% of Americans keep to their resolutions.
True ☐ **False** ☐

3 Joanna has a resolution for every day of the year.
True ☐ **False** ☐

4 Joanna is going to climb a mountain on July 23.
True ☐ **False** ☐

5 Joanna is going to swim with dolphins.
True ☐ **False** ☐

119

36.6 KEY LANGUAGE "BY" WITH TIME WORDS AND PHRASES

"By" followed by a noun or time phrase means something will happen at some point before that time.

"Going to" follows the verb "to be."

I am going to paint the house by June.

NOW   JUNE

36.7 FURTHER EXAMPLES "BY" WITH TIME WORDS AND PHRASES

You are going to write to the person between now and next weekend.

I am going to write to you by next weekend.

I am going to get fit by this time next year.

You are going to get fit by the same date the following year.

36.8 READ JACK'S RESOLUTIONS, THEN WRITE ABOUT THEM USING "GOING TO"

He is going to tidy his house by the weekend.

Jack's January Resolutions

- Tidy my house by the weekend.
- Paint my bedroom by the end of this month.
- Join a gym by this time next month.
- Reserve a vacation by the end of March.
- Get fit by the summer.
- Buy a new car by December.

1 _____

2 _____

3 _____

4 _____

5 _____

36.9 REWRITE THE SENTENCES, PUTTING THE WORDS IN THE CORRECT ORDER

| end of | are | next year. | Aziz and Julie | get married | going to | by the |

Aziz and Julie are going to get married by the end of next year.

① | by | going to | buy | Tim | a | October. | is | new boat |

_____

② | are | going to | on the | Sally and Jane | vacation | go on | weekend. |

_____

③ | next year. | by | going to | write | a book | I am | this time |

_____

④ | run | are | tomorrow. | a | marathon | going to | We |

_____

🔊

36.10 LISTEN TO THE AUDIO, THEN MATCH EACH PERSON TO THE CORRECT ACTIVITY AND TIME PHRASE

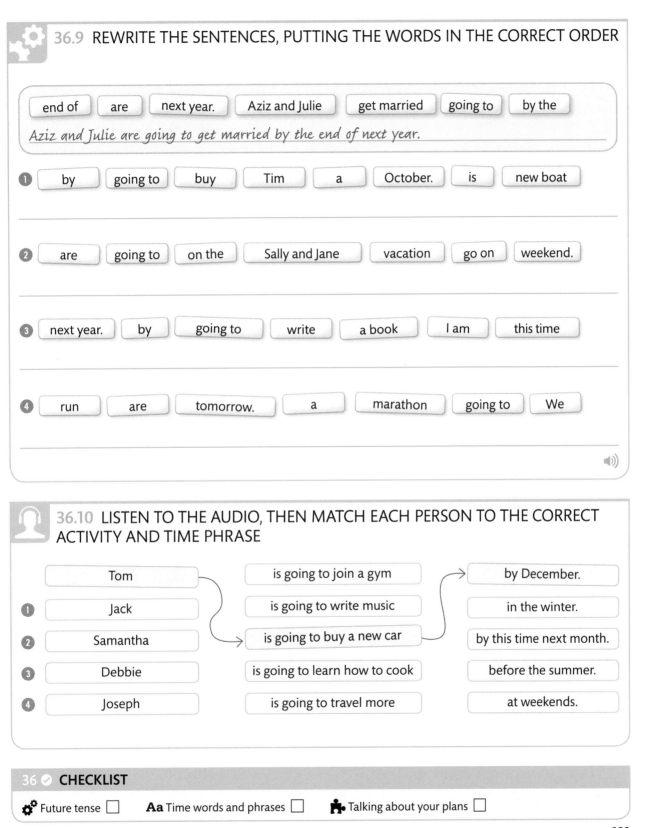

Tom	is going to join a gym	by December.
Jack ①	is going to write music	in the winter.
Samantha ②	is going to buy a new car	by this time next month.
Debbie ③	is going to learn how to cook	before the summer.
Joseph ④	is going to travel more	at weekends.

36 ✓ CHECKLIST

⚙ Future tense ☐   **Aa** Time words and phrases ☐   🧩 Talking about your plans ☐

37 What's going to happen

Use the future with "going to" to make a prediction about the future when there is evidence in the present moment to back up that prediction.

⚙ **New language** The future with "going to"
Aa Vocabulary Prediction verbs
🧩 **New skill** Predicting future events

37.1 KEY LANGUAGE "GOING TO" FOR FUTURE EVENTS

This form of the future is formed using "to be" + "going to" + the base form of the verb.

Use "going to" to give your prediction.

Look at those clouds. It's going to rain soon.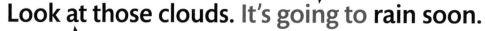

Evidence in the present moment means that you can make a prediction.

🔊

37.2 FURTHER EXAMPLES "GOING TO" FOR FUTURE EVENTS

Oh no! She's going to slip and fall over.

The hill is too steep. Jon is going to crash!

She studies a lot. She's going to pass her exam.

Look! The waiter is going to drop those plates.

They're going to break a window.

Joe fell asleep in the exam. He's going to fail.

He's wearing a raincoat, so he's not going to get wet.

🔊

37.3 FILL IN THE GAPS PUTTING THE VERBS IN THE FUTURE WITH "GOING TO"

Kim doesn't study very hard. She _____*is going to fail*_____ (✗ fail) her exams.

1 Watch out! You _____ (step into) that puddle.

2 The dog _____ (not eat) its food. I think it's sick.

3 Oh no! She _____ (fall off) the ladder.

4 John is terrible at golf! He _____ (not win) the tournament.

5 It's very windy! His umbrella _____ (blow away).

6 You're carrying too much. You _____ (drop) everything.

37.4 REWRITE THE SENTENCES, CORRECTING THE ERRORS

The traffic is moving very slowly. I **are** going to be late for work.
The traffic is moving very slowly. I am going to be late for work.

1 John and Jill are putting their coats on. They **is** going to leave now.

_____

2 I saw the weather forecast. It **are** going to snow this afternoon.

_____

3 It's my birthday, so I **is** going to get a present from my husband.

_____

4 Larry and John have gone home to get their tennis rackets. They **is** going to play tennis.

_____

37.5 READ THE SCHOOL REPORT, THEN FILL IN THE GAPS USING "GOING TO" OR "NOT GOING TO"

Marco is ___*going to*___ pass his history exam.

1 He is _____ be in the next Olympics.

2 Marco is _____ study art at college.

3 He is _____ be the main character in a musical.

4 Marco is _____ fail his English exam.

5 He is _____ play soccer next weekend.

Report: Marco Di Stefano

English 33%	Marco needs to work harder at Engl[i]. He is predicted not to pass this exam.
History 95%	This is Marco's best subject. He doesn['t] have any problems and will do well in the exam.
Music 25%	Marco doesn't like to sing and doesn't play a musical instrument.
Art 92%	Marco loves this subject and is very good at it. He has an offer from Rome Art College and wants to study art.
Gym 55%	This is not Marco's best subject, but he is a member of the soccer team. They play every weekend.

Aa 37.6 READ THE CLUES AND WRITE THE ANSWERS IN THE CORRECT PLACES ON THE GRID

1 Pick up those toys. Someone is going to _____ them.

2 You're going to _____ someone if you skateboard on the sidewalk.

3 Jo left her exam too early. She's going to _____ .

4 Ben is clever. He's going to easily _____ his test.

5 That wall is too high. He is going to _____ his leg if he jumps off it.

fall over   fail   crash into   break   pass

37.7 LOOK AT THE PICTURES, THEN FILL IN THE GAPS USING THE WORDS IN THE PANEL, SPEAKING OUT LOUD

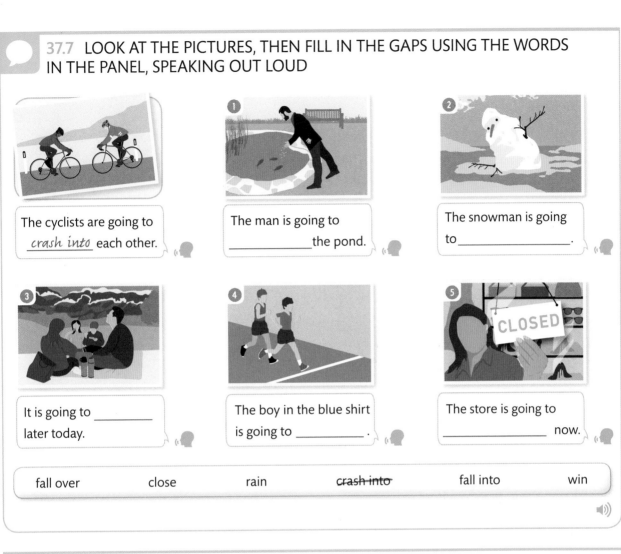

The cyclists are going to _crash into_ each other.

① The man is going to _____ the pond.

② The snowman is going to _____.

③ It is going to _____ later today.

④ The boy in the blue shirt is going to _____.

⑤ The store is going to _____ now.

| fall over | close | rain | ~~crash into~~ | fall into | win |

37.8 USE THE CHART TO CREATE 12 CORRECT SENTENCES AND SAY THEM OUT LOUD

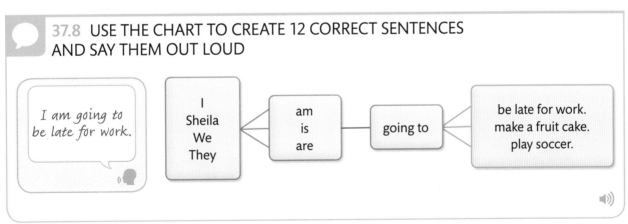

I am going to be late for work.

| I Sheila We They | am is are | going to | be late for work. make a fruit cake. play soccer. |

37 ✓ CHECKLIST

⚙ Future tense with "going to" ☐   **Aa** Prediction verbs ☐   🧩 Predicting future events ☐

38.1 ANIMALS

insect

fish

bird

bear

rhino

buffalo

camel

lion

tiger

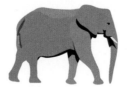

elephant

monkey

giraffe

kangaroo

bull

cow

mouse

 rat

 eagle

 snake

 lizard

 frog

 shark

 whale

 dolphin

 crab

 octopus

 turtle

 crocodile

 bee

 fly

 spider

 butterfly

39 Making predictions

You can use the verb "will" to talk about future events in English. This form of the future tense has a slightly different meaning from futures using "going to."

⚙ **New language** The future with "will"
Aa Vocabulary Prediction words
New skill Saying what you think will happen

39.1 KEY LANGUAGE THE FUTURE WITH "WILL"

Use "will" to say what you think will happen in the future when you don't have firm evidence for your prediction.

That new movie is great. They will love it.

You think the other people will love the movie, but you don't have firm evidence.

39.2 FURTHER EXAMPLES THE FUTURE WITH "WILL"

 Jane will like the new house. It's really nice.

 It'll rain every day this summer.

You can also say "he'll not," but "won't" is more common in US English.

In negative sentences, "not" goes between "will" and the base form of the verb.

 We will not get home before midnight.

He won't be late for work again this year.

In spoken English, you normally use the contracted form of "will."

 They'll enjoy their holiday in Venice.

 She'll be really angry when she finds out.

39.3 HOW TO FORM THE FUTURE WITH "WILL"

"Will" is a modal verb, so its form doesn't change with the subject.

SUBJECT	"WILL"	BASE FORM OF VERB	REST OF SENTENCE
She	will	love	the new movie.

39.4 FILL IN THE GAPS USING THE FUTURE WITH "WILL" OR "WILL NOT"

You _____*will love*_____ (love) my new sweater.

❶ John _____ (not eat) pizza.

❷ Maria _____ (enjoy) the new dance class.

❸ Susie and Bella _____ (be) early for work this week.

❹ The children _____ (not understand) this information.

🔊

39.5 READ THE NOTE AND REWRITE THE HIGHLIGHTED PHRASES USING PRONOUNS AND CONTRACTED "WILL" WITH FUTURE VERBS

He'll buy pizzas.

❶ _____

❷ _____

❸ _____

❹ _____

❺ _____

Hi Jim,
What do you want us to bring to movie night? Ben will buy pizzas because he always does. John will bring chocolates and Mary will make a salad. As usual, David won't bring anything. I will bring drinks, and Lillian and Jo will buy cheese.
Is that OK?
Sandy

39.6 LISTEN TO THE AUDIO AND MATCH THE QUESTIONS TO THE CORRECT ANSWERS

Who will clean the house?   Jenny's brother will do it.

❶ Who will find the party music?   Jenny's mother will do it.

❷ Who will bring the party games?   Jenny's sister will do it.

❸ Who will bake a birthday cake?   Sam will do it.

❹ Who will cook the food?   Marsha will do it.

39.7 KEY LANGUAGE "THINK" WITH "WILL"

If you're not sure about something, you can begin a sentence with "I think." This shows you are giving your opinion.

You're not certain.

"That" is not essential to the sentence, and it's often left out.

We think that he'll like the play.

39.8 HOW TO FORM "THINK" WITH "WILL"

SUBJECT	"THINK"	"THAT"	SUBJECT + "WILL"	VERB	REST OF SENTENCE
We	think	**that**	he'll	like	the play.

"That" is often left out.

39.9 FURTHER EXAMPLES SENTENCES WITH "THINK" AND "WILL"

I think that we'll have enough food for the party.

He thinks it'll be a great show tonight.

It's cold outside, but we don't think it'll snow today.

To make the sentence negative, add "do not" or "don't" before "think."

She doesn't think she'll get that job at the bank.

39.10 MATCH THE SENTENCES TO THE CORRECT PREDICTIONS

Max cooks great meals at home.

1 Diana works very hard.

2 Chiara loves traveling.

3 Carl failed his driver's test again.

4 Georgia can't sing very well.

I think she'll pass her exams.

I don't think she'll be in the musical.

I think he'll become a fantastic chef.

I think she'll enjoy visiting Rome.

I don't think he'll ever pass it.

39.11 KEY LANGUAGE "GOING TO" AND "WILL"

Use "going to" when you have evidence for a prediction. Use "will" when a prediction is an opinion without evidence.

You are predicting this, but you don't have firm evidence.

I think Number 5 will win.

Look, Number 5 is going to win.

You are predicting this based on firm evidence.

 39.12 LOOK AT THE PICTURES, THEN SAY THE SENTENCES OUT LOUD, FILLING IN THE GAPS USING THE PHRASES IN THE PANEL

Lily is going to _____ the fence.

Bob is going to _____ all his dinner.

It is going to _____ this afternoon.

The dog will _____ these leftovers.

The car is going to _____ left.

John thinks he will _____ tonight.

eat	jump	turn	go out	eat	snow

---

39 ✓ CHECKLIST

⚙ The future with "will" ☐   **Aa** Prediction words ☐   🧩 Saying what you think will happen ☐

40 Making quick decisions

You can use "will" to talk about the future in two ways: when you make a prediction without evidence, and when you make a quick decision to do something.

⚙ **New language** Quick decisions with "will"
Aa Vocabulary Decision words
🧩 **New skill** Talking about future actions

40.1 KEY LANGUAGE QUICK DECISIONS WITH "WILL"

If you suddenly decide to do something while you're speaking, use "will" to say what you're going to do.

Oh, it's raining!
I'll take my umbrella.

"Will" shows you have just made the decision.

40.2 FURTHER EXAMPLES QUICK DECISIONS WITH "WILL"

Contracted form of "will not."

It's midnight, so I won't walk home through the park.

This apple is delicious. I'll have another one.

40.3 KEY LANGUAGE "SO / IN THAT CASE"

Use "so" or the expression "in that case" to link a situation and the decision you make as a result of that situation.

SITUATION   DECISION

There's no juice, so I'll have water.

The car won't start. In that case we'll walk.

SITUATION   DECISION

40.4 MATCH THE BEGINNINGS OF THE SENTENCES TO THE CORRECT ENDINGS

There's no bread,

① It's my birthday,

② I forgot my swimming trunks,

③ I don't have any money,

④ I can't find my train ticket,

so I won't go in the water.

so I won't go shopping.

so I'll get the bus.

so I'll go to the supermarket.

so I'll cut the cake.

40.5 LISTEN TO THE AUDIO, THEN NUMBER THE PICTURES IN THE ORDER THEY ARE DESCRIBED

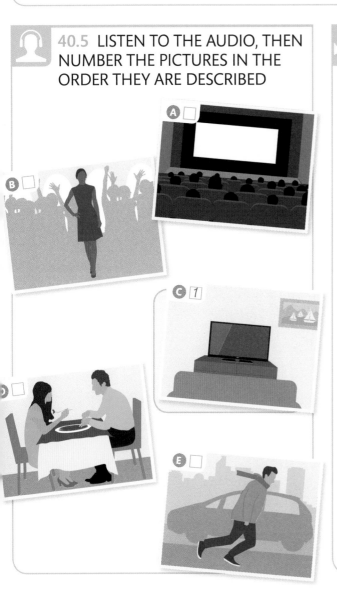

A ☐

B ☐

C ☑ 1

E ☐

40.6 FILL IN THE GAPS USING THE WORDS IN THE PANEL

Wow! It's really sunny outside.

In that case I'll ___wear___ a hat.

① Oh dear. There are no trains today.

In that case we'll _____ by bus.

② There isn't any coffee in the kitchen.

In that case I'll _____ tea.

③ Oh no! The restaurant is closed.

In that case we'll _____ at home.

④ There's nothing good on TV tonight.

In that case I'll _____ music.

listen to   ~~wear~~

go   have   eat

133

40.7 KEY LANGUAGE "THINK" WITH "WILL"

You can use "think" with "will" to show that your decision is something you are considering.

I'm tired. I **think** I'll go to bed.

↳ You are deciding now.
You're not completely sure.

40.8 FURTHER EXAMPLES "THINK" WITH "WILL"

There are lots of options on the menu. I think we'll have the fish.

There are lots of bands to see, but I think I'll watch the rock band.

This movie is terrible. I think I'll leave before the end.

It's getting really hot outside. I think I'll put my shorts on.

40.9 READ THE TEXT MESSAGES AND ANSWER THE QUESTIONS

Two friends will buy her flowers.
True ☐ **False** ✓

❶ One friend will take her to a restaurant.
True ☐ **False** ☐

❷ One friend will have a party for her.
True ☐ **False** ☐

❸ One friend will get her ballet tickets.
True ☐ **False** ☐

❹ Two friends will take her shopping.
True ☐ **False** ☐

❺ One friend will make her a birthday cake.
True ☐ **False** ☐

❻ One friend will buy her a DVD.
True ☐ **False** ☐

Jo

It's Jeanie's birthday this weekend. Do you know what we can do for her, Sally?

Sure, Jo. I think I'll get her some flowers and a DVD.

Great. I think I'll take her shopping and buy her some clothes. What will James do?

James will have a party for her at his house on Tuesday.

Perfect. John will cook the food and bake her a cake.

Oh, and I think Jemima will buy Jeanie some movie tickets and take her shopping.

40.10 SAY THE SENTENCES OUT LOUD, FILLING IN THE GAPS USING THE PHRASES IN THE PANEL

The TV is broken. What will you do tonight?

I think I'll _read a book_ .

3 Jo is busy, so who will you play tennis with?

I think I'll _____ .

1 There's no juice. What do you want to drink?

I think I'll _____ .

4 Which TV show do you want to see?

I think I'll _____ .

2 What time are you leaving work?

I think I'll _____ .

5 Where do you want to go now?

I think I'll _____ .

play with Cassie   have milk   read a book   leave at 6:30pm   go home   watch the news

---

40 ✓ CHECKLIST

⚙ Quick decisions with "will" ☐   **Aa** Decision words ☐   🧩 Talking about future actions ☐

↻ REVIEW THE ENGLISH YOU HAVE LEARNED IN UNITS 35–40

NEW LANGUAGE	SAMPLE SENTENCE	☑	UNIT
FUTURE TENSE WITH PRESENT CONTINUOUS	At the moment, Dave is working, but tomorrow he is playing golf.	☐	35.1, 35.3, 35.6
"GOING TO" FOR FUTURE PLANS	I'm going to buy a new car. We are going to exercise tonight.	☐	36.1, 36.6
FUTURE TENSE WITH "GOING TO"	Look at those clouds. It's going to rain soon.	☐	37.1, 37.2
FUTURE TENSE WITH "WILL"	That new movie is great. They will love it.	☐	39.1, 39.7, 39.11
QUICK DECISIONS WITH "WILL"	Oh, it's raining! I'll take my umbrella.	☐	40.1, 40.4, 40.7

41 Future possibilities

Use "might" to show you're not sure if you'll do something. It's a possibility and you don't want to say that you "will" or you "won't."

⚙ **New language** Using "might"
Aa Vocabulary Activities, food, and pastimes
🧩 **New skill** Talking about future possibilities

41.1 KEY LANGUAGE "MIGHT" WITH FUTURE POSSIBILITIES

"Will" and "won't" describe things that are certain to happen or certain not to happen. Use "might" to show that something is not certain.

Negative
I won't have a vacation. **I don't have enough money.**

Possible
I might have a vacation. **I have some money.**

Positive
I will have a vacation because **I have lots of money.**

🔊

41.2 FURTHER EXAMPLES "MIGHT" WITH FUTURE POSSIBILITIES

To form the negative, add "not" between "might" and the verb. In UK English, it can be shortened to "mightn't."

He might not go to Rome this year. He doesn't know yet.

I might speak English at the party tonight as there are British people coming.

🔊

> **TIP**
> "Might" isn't normally used in questions.

41.3 HOW TO FORM "MIGHT" WITH FUTURE POSSIBILITIES

SUBJECT	"MIGHT"	MAIN VERB	REST OF SENTENCE
I / You He / She / It We / They	might might not mightn't	have	a vacation.

As with all modal verbs, "might" doesn't change with the subject.

Use the base form of the main verb.

41.4 REWRITE THE SENTENCES, PUTTING THE WORDS IN THE CORRECT ORDER

| She | to | might | party. | my | come |

She might come to my party.

❶ | dad | My | me | give | some money. | might |

_____

❷ | might | Helen | test. | driving | pass | her |

_____

❸ | bar. | might | I | not | a chocolate | eat |

_____

❹ | They | not | have | party. | a | might |

_____

41.5 REWRITE THE HIGHLIGHTED PHRASES, CORRECTING THE ERRORS

Hi Bill,

I'm excited about our hiking trip on Saturday. It might rains in the afternoon so we wills go in the morning. I'll brings some water, but I willn't bring any food. We mights wanting to stop at one of the pubs on our walk. What do you think?

See you this weekend,

Matt

It might rain

❶ _____

❷ _____

❸ _____

❹ _____

41.6 FILL IN THE GAPS USING "WON'T," "MIGHT," AND "WILL"

NEGATIVE	POSSIBLE	POSITIVE
I won't buy a computer.	I might buy a computer.	I will buy a computer.
❶ _____	_____	They will make dinner.
❷ _____	He might be late again.	_____
❸ You won't remember that.	_____	_____
❹ _____	She might become a teacher.	_____
❺ _____	_____	We will win the game!
❻ The dog won't eat this food.	_____	_____

41.7 KEY LANGUAGE "MIGHT" WITH UNCERTAINTY

You can use other phrases along with "might" to emphasize that you are uncertain about something.

 I might **go to town.** I'm not sure.

I don't know. I might **have more pizza.**

Aa 41.8 MATCH THE QUESTIONS TO THE ANSWERS

When are you going to clean your room?

1 Where will you live next year?

2 What will you do before you start college?

3 How much money are you taking on vacation?

I don't know. I might live in Boston.

I might get a summer job. I'm not sure.

I might do it this afternoon. I'm not sure.

I'm not sure. I might take about $300.

41.9 LISTEN TO THE AUDIO AND ANSWER THE QUESTIONS

Will John go to work today?
Yes, he will. ☐
He might. ☑
No, he won't. ☐

1 Is Mel going to the party this evening?
Yes, she is. ☐
She might. ☐
No, she isn't. ☐

2 Are Donna and Elise going swimming today?
Yes, they are. ☐
They might. ☐
No, they're not. ☐

3 Will Elliot be late for the concert?
Yes, he will. ☐
He might. ☐
No, he won't. ☐

4 Will Elsa study English?
Yes, she will. ☐
She might. ☐
No, she won't. ☐

5 Will Delilah travel by bus today?
Yes, she will. ☐
She might. ☐
No, she won't. ☐

41.10 SAY THE SENTENCES OUT LOUD USING "WILL," "MIGHT," AND "WON'T"

	POSITIVE	POSSIBLE	NEGATIVE
ABAN	go on vacation this year	① learn French	② run a marathon
NADIYA	③ become a doctor	④ write a book	⑤ do a bungee jump
JACK	⑥ get a dog	⑦ buy a motorcycle	⑧ move house

Aban will go on vacation this year.

①

②

③

④

⑤

⑥

⑦

⑧

42 Giving advice

If someone has a problem, one of the ways that you can give advice is by using the modal verb "should."

⚙ **New language** "Should"
Aa Vocabulary Advice
🧩 **New skill** Giving advice

42.1 KEY LANGUAGE "SHOULD" TO GIVE ADVICE

"Should" shows that you think this is the best thing to do.

It's very sunny. You should wear a hat.

"Should" comes before the advice.

42.2 FURTHER EXAMPLES "SHOULD" TO GIVE ADVICE

It might rain. You should take your umbrella.

For a negative, add "not" between "should" and the main verb.

There's ice on the roads. You should not drive tonight.

"Should not" can be shortened to "shouldn't."

You're sick. You shouldn't go to work today.

42.3 HOW TO FORM "SHOULD" TO GIVE ADVICE

SUBJECT	"SHOULD"	MAIN VERB	REST OF SENTENCE
You	should	wear	a hat.

"Should" is a modal verb, so it stays the same no matter what the subject is.

"Should" is followed by the base form of the verb.

42.4 REWRITE THE SENTENCES, CORRECTING THE ERRORS

> Kim should arrives on time.
> *Kim should arrive on time.*

1 You shouldn't opens this door.

_____

2 She shoulds to play the guitar every day.

_____

3 He shouldn't wears that tie with that shirt.

_____

4 You should to take a tablet twice a day.

_____

5 They shouldn't to rides their bikes here.

_____

🔊

42.5 LOOK AT THE PICTURES AND CROSS OUT THE INCORRECT WORDS IN THE SENTENCES TO GIVE GOOD ADVICE

Kim ~~should~~ / should not try to get on the train.

3 Shoppers should / shouldn't email.

1 We should / shouldn't swim at this beach.

4 They should / should not walk on the ice.

2 People should / should not be quiet in the library.

5 You should / shouldn't drive too fast.

🔊

Aa 42.6 MATCH THE PROBLEMS TO THE ADVICE

My plants are dying.	You should sell some of them.
1 I've got too many clothes.	You should get more sleep.
2 I eat too much junk food.	You should eat more fruit.
3 I don't know my neighbors.	You should water them.
4 I feel tired all the time.	You should join a gym.
5 I need more exercise.	You should have a block party.
6 I'm so lonely.	You should go shopping.
7 I've nothing to wear tonight.	You should get a dog.

42.7 LISTEN TO THE AUDIO AND MARK THE CORRECT PIECE OF ADVICE FOR EACH PROBLEM

To get to work tomorrow, James should...
- **leave early** ☐
- **take the bus** ☐
- **walk.** ☑

1 On the trip, people should...
- **bring $10** ☐
- **complete a form** ☐
- **be on time.** ☐

2 Maya says Matt should first...
- **clean up** ☐
- **finish his work** ☐
- **eat dinner.** ☐

3 Sheila's busy at work. Martin says she should...
- **go to bed later** ☐
- **work on the weekend** ☐
- **get up earlier.** ☐

4 Atif's sister thinks he should...
- **buy a new computer** ☐
- **use a friend's computer** ☐
- **write emails on his phone.** ☐

5 In the exam, students should...
- **be quiet** ☐
- **read all the information** ☐
- **speak clearly.** ☐

42.8 SAY THE SENTENCES OUT LOUD, FILLING IN THE GAPS USING "SHOULD" OR "SHOULDN'T"

He ___shouldn't___ go climbing in the rain.

3 You _____ eat anything in a laboratory.

1 People _____ visit the library more often.

4 You _____ go through that blue door.

2 People _____ have a shower before swimming.

5 Students _____ speak during their exams.

---

42 ✓ CHECKLIST

⚙ "Should" ☐   **Aa** Advice ☐   🧩 Giving advice ☐

43 Making suggestions

You can use the modal verb "could" to offer suggestions. "Could" is not as strong as "should." It communicates gentle advice.

🔧 **New language** "Could" for suggestions
Aa Vocabulary Advice
🧩 **New skill** Making suggestions

43.1 KEY LANGUAGE "COULD" FOR SUGGESTIONS

"Could" is often used to suggest a solution to a problem. It introduces possibilities but not preferences.

I hate my car!

Well, you could get a new one!

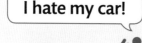

"Could" means that the action is a possibility; a choice that might solve the problem.

43.2 FURTHER EXAMPLES "COULD" FOR SUGGESTIONS

You could study **science in college.**

We could learn **English in Canada next year.**

They could buy **a bigger house with a yard.**

You could get **a job at that new restaurant in town.**

43.3 HOW TO FORM "COULD" FOR SUGGESTIONS

SUBJECT	"COULD"	VERB	REST OF SENTENCE
You	could	get	a new car.

"Could" is a modal verb, so it doesn't change with the subject.

The main verb goes in its base form.

43.4 MATCH THE PROBLEMS TO THE CORRECT SUGGESTIONS

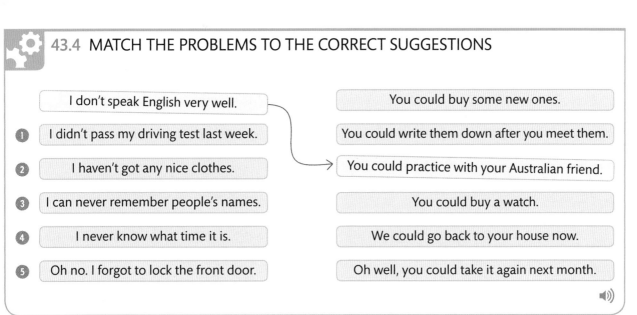

I don't speak English very well.

① I didn't pass my driving test last week.

② I haven't got any nice clothes.

③ I can never remember people's names.

④ I never know what time it is.

⑤ Oh no. I forgot to lock the front door.

You could buy some new ones.

You could write them down after you meet them.

You could practice with your Australian friend.

You could buy a watch.

We could go back to your house now.

Oh well, you could take it again next month.

43.5 CHOOSE THE CORRECT SUGGESTIONS FROM THE PANEL, THEN SAY THE SENTENCES OUT LOUD

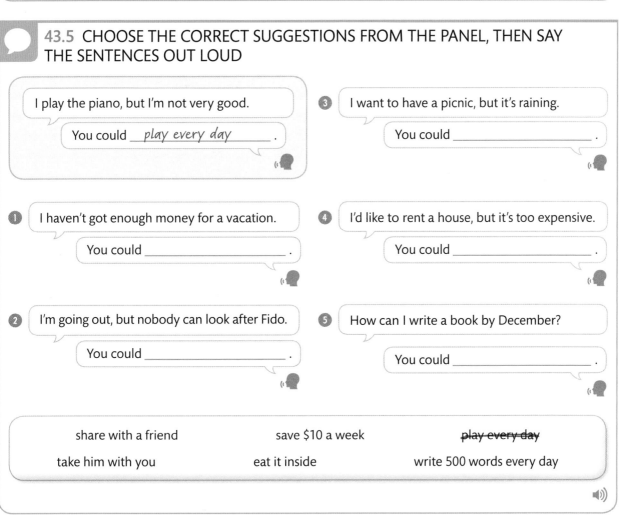

I play the piano, but I'm not very good.

You could __play every day__.

③ I want to have a picnic, but it's raining.

You could _____.

① I haven't got enough money for a vacation.

You could _____.

④ I'd like to rent a house, but it's too expensive.

You could _____.

② I'm going out, but nobody can look after Fido.

You could _____.

⑤ How can I write a book by December?

You could _____.

share with a friend   save $10 a week   ~~play every day~~

take him with you   eat it inside   write 500 words every day

43.6 KEY LANGUAGE USING "COULD" AND "OR" FOR SUGGESTIONS

When people give suggestions using "could," they often give more than one option to choose from.

Our friends are coming over for dinner, but the oven's broken.

We could make a salad or we could order a pizza.

Use "or" to give an alternative suggestion.

43.7 FURTHER EXAMPLES USING "COULD" AND "OR" FOR SUGGESTIONS

I can't drive, but I want to travel along the coast.

You could take **a bus** or travel **in a friend's car.**

You don't have to repeat the modal verb "could" after "or."

What should I wear to Jan's wedding?

You could wear **your new dress** or a ski

If the main verb is the same for both suggestions, you don't repeat it after "or."

43.8 USE THE PHRASES TO WRITE SUGGESTIONS USING "COULD" AND "OR"

You can't sleep at night. You could _____ *read a book* _____ or _____ *have a hot drink* _____ .

1. You don't know what to do for the summer. You could _____ or _____ .

2. What are you going to make for dinner tonight? You could cook _____ or _____ .

3. You want to be a better tennis player. You could _____ or _____ .

4. You can't wake up in the mornings. You could _____ or _____ .

~~read a book~~   get a job   ~~have a hot drink~~   travel   chicken   set an alarm

have some lessons   go to bed earlier   beef   play more often

146

43.9 LISTEN TO THE AUDIO AND MARK THE TWO SUGGESTIONS GIVEN TO SOLVE EACH PROBLEM

Anya can't understand her English teacher very well. She could...
ask him to speak slowly. ☐ **ask for notes on the lesson.** ☑ **record the lesson.** ☑

① Jim hasn't got time to do the chores at home. He could...
get his children to help. ☐ **get a cleaner.** ☐ **not worry about it.** ☐

② Mandy needs to get a new job. She could...
look in the newspaper. ☐ **ask friends.** ☐ **look at a website.** ☐

③ Some students aren't very good at writing in English. They could...
read more English books. ☐ **write in English every day.** ☐ **email a new friend in English.** ☐

④ It's hard to find time to exercise. People could...
take the stairs. ☐ **take the elevator.** ☐ **walk to the store.** ☐

43 ⊘ CHECKLIST

⚙ "Could" for suggestions ☐   **Aa** Advice ☐   🏃 Making suggestions ☐

↻ REVIEW THE ENGLISH YOU HAVE LEARNED IN UNITS 41–43

NEW LANGUAGE	SAMPLE SENTENCE	☑	UNIT
USING "MIGHT" WITH FUTURE POSSIBILITIES	I might have a vacation.	☐	41.1
USING "MIGHT" WITH UNCERTAINTY	I might go to town. I'm not sure. I don't know. I might have some pizza.	☐	41.7
USING "SHOULD" TO GIVE ADVICE	It's very sunny. You should wear a hat.	☐	42.1
USING "SHOULDN'T" TO GIVE ADVICE	You're sick. You shouldn't go to work today.	☐	42.1
USING "COULD" FOR SUGGESTIONS	You could get a new car.	☐	43.1
USING "OR" FOR SUGGESTIONS	We could make a salad or order a pizza.	☐	43.6

44.1 HOUSEHOLD CHORES

clean the windows

sweep the floor

scrub the floor

mop the floor

vacuum the carpet

dust

take out the garbage (US)
take out the rubbish (UK)

tidy

go to the store (US)
go to the shops (UK)

buy groceries

chop vegetables

cook dinner

set the table

clear the table

do the dishes (US)
do the washing up (UK)

dry the dishes

load the
dishwasher

do the laundry (US)
do the washing (UK)

hang clothes (US)
hang out the
washing (UK)

do the ironing

fold clothes

make the bed

change the sheets

do the gardening

mow the lawn

water the plants

wash the car

paint a room

hang a picture

walk the dog

feed the pets

mend the fence

45 Around the house

You can use the present perfect form of a verb to talk about something that has happened in the past and has consequences in the present.

⚙ **New language** The present perfect
Aa Vocabulary Household chores
🧩 **New skill** Talking about the recent past

45.1 KEY LANGUAGE THE PRESENT PERFECT

Use the present perfect to describe something that has happened in the past and which has a result in the present moment.

TIP
Form regular past participles in the same way that you form the past simple, by adding "ed" to the base form of the verb.

"Just" means that the action has happened recently.

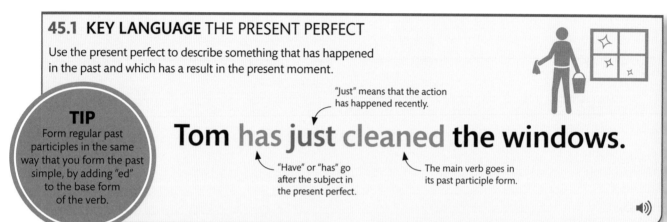

Tom has just cleaned the windows.

"Have" or "has" go after the subject in the present perfect.

The main verb goes in its past participle form.

◀))

45.2 FURTHER EXAMPLES THE PRESENT PERFECT

Look! I've just cooked **dinner.**

You haven't cleared **the table. It's a mess!**

John has just washed **the dishes.**

Have you cleaned up **your bedroom?**

◀))

45.3 HOW TO FORM THE PRESENT PERFECT

SUBJECT + "HAVE" / "HAS"	"JUST"	PAST PARTICIPLE	OBJECT
I have	just	cleaned	the windows.

To make the present perfect, use "have" or "has" with the past participle of the verb.

45.4 KEY LANGUAGE FORMING IRREGULAR PAST PARTICIPLES

There are no rules for forming irregular past participles, but some irregular past participles have similar endings.

I am ➡ I've been

you eat ➡ you've eaten

they see ➡ they've seen

we do ➡ we've done

I put ➡ I've put

you leave ➡ you've left

they keep ➡ they've kept

we hear ➡ we've heard

45.5 FILL IN THE GAPS BY PUTTING THE VERBS INTO THE PRESENT PERFECT

I _have cleaned_ (clean) the kitchen.

1 We _____ (not mop) the floor.

2 Tim _____ (leave) the door open.

3 You _____ (change) the sheets.

4 Sheila _____ (eat) her dinner.

5 Dad _____ (not paint) the fence.

6 I _____ (vacuum) the living room.

7 Aziz _____ (water) the plants.

45.6 FILL IN THE GAPS TO WRITE EACH SENTENCE THREE DIFFERENT WAYS

He has washed his clothes.	He hasn't washed his clothes.	Has he washed his clothes?
1 They have cleaned the car.		
2		Have you mopped the floor?
3	I haven't taken the garbage out.	
4 You have painted the house.		
5		Has John cooked dinner?

151

Aa 45.7 FIND EIGHT REGULAR AND IRREGULAR PAST PARTICIPLES AND WRITE THEM NEXT TO THE CORRECT VERBS

```
C L E A T E N N E N H L
L V P C H A D U W Z S N
O Q D O N E P Y T I E S
S B Z K Y A X(G O N E)F
E H Q L X G J A T D N K
D E B E E N S E H A K E
K A G Y H T F L Z J K J
E D W T N G K E P T Z L
```

1. go = _gone_
2. have = _____
3. close = _____
4. eat = _____
5. am = _____
6. keep = _____
7. see = _____
8. do = _____

45.8 REWRITE THE SENTENCES, CORRECTING THE ERRORS

> Ellen have left her keys at home.
> _Ellen has left her keys at home._

1. We have cook dinner for you.
   _____

2. Ben and Ellen has gone to the supermarket.
   _____

3. The children have see the movie.
   _____

4. Sheila has clean the bathroom.
   _____

5. The dog haven't eaten all its food.
   _____

6. They've be to the mall to buy you a present.
   _____

◀))

45.9 LISTEN TO THE AUDIO AND ANSWER THE QUESTIONS

Adam and Becky are getting ready to have a party.

> Has Adam cleaned the bathroom?
> **Yes, he has.** ✓ **No, he hasn't.** ☐

1. Have they bought enough drinks?
   Yes, they have. ☐ **No, they haven't.** ☐

2. Has Becky put the chicken in the oven?
   Yes, she has. ☐ **No, she hasn't.** ☐

3. Has Adam talked to his sister?
   Yes, he has. ☐ **No, he hasn't.** ☐

4. Has Adam's sister sent him a present?
   Yes, she has. ☐ **No, she hasn't.** ☐

5. Has Adam moved his car?
   Yes, he has. ☐ **No, he hasn't.** ☐

45.10 REWRITE THESE VERBS AS PAST PARTICIPLES

tidy = *tidied*

1. clean = _____
2. wash = _____
3. cook = _____
4. change = _____
5. mop = _____
6. walk = _____
7. clear = _____
8. brush = _____

45.11 SAY THE SENTENCES OUT LOUD, FILLING IN THE GAPS BY PUTTING THE VERBS FROM THE PANEL IN THE PRESENT PERFECT

Mark has *washed* the dishes.

1. The children have _____ the car.

2. The cat has _____ all its food.

3. Jemma has _____ the window.

4. Jill has _____ her desk.

5. Paul has _____ his wallet on top of the car.

| clean | ~~wash~~ | tidy | break | leave | eat |

46 Events in your life

Both the present perfect and the past simple can be used to talk about things that happened in the past, but you use them differently.

⚙ **New language** The present perfect
Aa Vocabulary Adventure sports
🧩 **New skill** Talking about past events

46.1 KEY LANGUAGE THE PRESENT PERFECT AND THE PAST SIMPLE

Use the past simple to talk about something that happened at a definite time. Use the present perfect when you don't specify a particular time.

Have you ever been to France?

Yes, I visited Paris in 2010.

You give a specific date, 2010, so use the past simple.

2010   NOW

You don't give a specific date, so use the present perfect.

Yes, I have visited Paris many times.

2003   2008   2010   2014   NOW

46.2 FURTHER EXAMPLES THE PRESENT PERFECT AND THE PAST SIMPLE

PAST SIMPLE	PRESENT PERFECT
I saw a great movie last week.	I haven't seen that movie.
Jo didn't climb Mount Fuji last year.	Saki has climbed Mount Fuji twice.
Madison ate too much last night.	Jack hasn't eaten curry before.

46.3 VOCABULARY ADVENTURE SPORTS

scuba diving   rock climbing   paragliding   windsurfing   bungee jumping   surfing

46.4 CROSS OUT THE INCORRECT WORDS IN EACH SENTENCE

Natalia **visited** / ~~has visited~~ China last year.

1 I love the movie *Casablanca*. I **watched** / have watched it more than nine times.

2 Our dog Rex **ate** / has eaten all Mary's birthday cake last night.

3 Jack **didn't visit** / hasn't visited the Colosseum when we were in Rome last year. He was too sick.

4 **Did you go** / Have you been to the swimming pool downtown yesterday?

46.5 SAY THE SENTENCES OUT LOUD, FILLING IN THE GAPS

Have you ever been surfing?

Yes, *I've been surfing* many times.

1 Has Chloe ever been bungee jumping?

Yes, _____ many times.

2 Has Liam ever visited Yosemite National Park?

Yes, _____ in 2014.

3 Have you ever seen *Gone with the Wind*?

Yes, _____ last night.

4 Have you ever been paragliding?

No, _____ .

5 Have any of your friends been scuba diving?

Yes, Mia _____ many times.

155

46.6 KEY LANGUAGE "BEEN / GONE"

You can use "be" and "go" in the present perfect to talk about your trips to places, but they have different meanings.

I haven't seen Joan recently. Where is she?

She's gone to Florida.

She is still in Florida.

Hi, Joan. You're looking well.

Yes, I've been to Florida.

She went to Florida, but now she is back home.

46.7 FURTHER EXAMPLES "BEEN / GONE"

Where's Ben?

He's gone to the mall.

Where's Ariana?

She's gone windsurfing.

You look relaxed.

Yes, we've been in Bermuda. We had a great time.

What's Julie doing?

She's been swimming and now she's doing her homework.

46.8 FILL IN THE GAPS USING "BEEN" OR "GONE"

I love Chicago. I've ___*been*___ there often.

1. Manuela and Giorgio have _____ to the movies. They're meeting you there.

2. There's lots of food in the fridge because Ayida's _____ to the supermarket.

3. I've _____ to the library. Look at all the books I have!

4. Mary and Joe have _____ to a nightclub. They'll be back after midnight.

46.9 READ THE POSTCARD AND WRITE THE VERBS UNDER THE CORRECT HEADINGS

PRESENT PERFECT

> we've seen

❶ _____

❷ _____

PAST SIMPLE

> we got

❶ _____

❷ _____

Hi Chris,
We're in Sydney! We got here five days ago and we've seen so much. On Monday, we visited the Sydney Opera House, and on Tuesday we went on a boat under Harbour Bridge. We haven't been to Bondi Beach yet, but I think we're going tomorrow. We've eaten some great food, too! Wish you were here.
Love,
Olivia x

46.10 LISTEN TO THE AUDIO AND ANSWER THE QUESTIONS

> Martin has been bungee jumping three times.
> **True** ☐ **False** ☑

❶ Sammy went to China in 2011.
True ☐ **False** ☐

❷ Nigel has never cooked a meal for visitors.
True ☐ **False** ☐

❸ Debra has been rock climbing many times.
True ☐ **False** ☐

❹ Andrew has never used a tablet before.
True ☐ **False** ☐

46.11 REWRITE THE SENTENCES, CORRECTING THE ERRORS

> I've **gone** windsurfing many times.
> _I've been windsurfing many times._

❶ She hasn't **be** to the circus.

_____

❷ I **meet** my best friend when I was six.

_____

❸ You **eat** all the chocolate last night.

_____

❹ He hasn't **try** paragliding.

_____

🔊

---

46 ✓ **CHECKLIST**

⚙ The present perfect ☐ | **Aa** Adventure sports ☐ | 🧩 Talking about past events ☐

47 Events in your year

One of the uses of the present perfect is to talk about events in a time period that hasn't finished. Use the past simple for a time period that is completed.

⚙ **New language** "Yet" and "already"
Aa Vocabulary Routines and chores
🧩 **New skill** Talking about the recent past

47.1 KEY LANGUAGE PRESENT PERFECT AND PAST SIMPLE

If the time period referred to is ongoing, use the present perfect. Use the past simple to talk about a completed event.

This year has not finished yet. Use the present perfect.

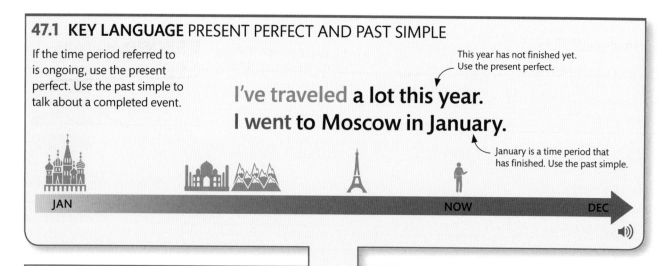

I've traveled a lot this year.
I went to Moscow in January.

January is a time period that has finished. Use the past simple.

JAN — NOW — DEC

47.2 FURTHER EXAMPLES PRESENT PERFECT AND PAST SIMPLE

 I haven't had any coffee this morning.

 The photocopier broke yesterday.

 I've had a lot of meetings today.

 My manager called me last night.

47.3 FILL IN THE GAPS BY PUTTING THE VERBS IN THE PRESENT PERFECT OR PAST SIMPLE

I'm flying to New York again tomorrow. I ___*have been*___ (be) there five times this year.

1 Alvita is very happy. She _____ (win) the prize for the best chocolate cake yesterday.

2 This is a great party. I _____ (meet) lots of really fun and interesting people.

3 Martha looks happy. She _____ (be) to the movies with Miles.

4 Mary can't drive. She _____ (fall) and _____ (break) her arm last week.

41 SPORT TODAY

TENNIS STAR'S DIFFICULT YEAR

Sarah Jackson speaks to our sports reporter.

Sarah Jackson is a tennis player from the US. She has won five tennis championships, but she hasn't played in any competitions this year.

"I haven't had a good year. I broke my leg in January and I didn't play tennis for three months. It was really painful and it took me a long time to get well."

There are four big competitions for tennis players, known as the Grand Slams: the Australian Open, the French Open, Wimbledon, and the US Open. Sarah has already missed two of them.

"It's difficult for tennis players. You want to do well in the big competitions, but sometimes you can't."

The next grand slam is Wimbledon, but Sarah isn't going to play this year. "It's sad, but I'm just not ready for Wimbledon at the moment."

But the year hasn't been all bad: "I don't usually go on vacation," she told us, "but in March I went to the Caribbean. I had a really good time and relaxed. I also ate some great food and went swimming."

How many tennis championships has Sarah won?

She has won five tennis championships.

3 How long didn't she play tennis for?

1 What hasn't Sarah done this year?

4 How many grand slams has Sarah missed this year?

2 What did Sarah do in January?

5 What did Sarah do in March this year?

159

47.5 KEY LANGUAGE "YET"

"Yet" means "until now." It shows that you have an intention to do something.

Have you ordered the pizzas?

No, I haven't ordered them yet.

You haven't ordered the pizzas, but you will order them later.

🔊

47.6 KEY LANGUAGE "ALREADY"

Use "already" when something has happened, possibly sooner than expected.

I'll order the pizzas now.

It's OK. I've already ordered **them.**

You've ordered the pizzas before the other person expected.

🔊

47.7 FURTHER EXAMPLES "ALREADY" AND "YET"

Has Rob cooked the dinner?

No, not yet.

You can use "yet" in short answers.

What time is Andrew going to get here?

He's already arrived.

🔊

47.8 MATCH THE QUESTIONS TO THE CORRECT ANSWERS

When is Phil going to get here? ——————————→ He's already arrived.

① Am I too late to play football?   No, the game hasn't started yet.

② Has Amy learned how to drive yet?   I've already done it.

③ Can you send an email to Rachel?   No, not yet.

④ Have you watched this movie?   Yes, I've already seen it.

🔊

47.9 LISTEN TO THE AUDIO AND ANSWER THE QUESTIONS

Sharon and Paul are getting ready to leave home and go on vacation.

Paul hasn't booked a taxi yet.
True ☐ **False** ✓

❸ Sharon hasn't checked if the dog is OK yet.
True ☐ **False** ☐

❶ Paul hasn't made the sandwiches yet.
True ☐ **False** ☐

❹ The dog has already been for a walk.
True ☐ **False** ☐

❷ Sharon has already called her mother.
True ☐ **False** ☐

❺ Sharon has already mailed her letter.
True ☐ **False** ☐

47.10 LOOK AT SANTIAGO'S "TO DO" LIST AND WRITE ANSWERS TO THE QUESTIONS AS FULL SENTENCES USING "ALREADY" AND "YET"

Has Santiago fed the cat yet?
Yes, he's already fed the cat.

Has he put out the garbage yet?
No, he hasn't put out the garbage yet.

To do list

~~Feed the cat~~
Put out the garbage
~~Clean the kitchen~~
~~Buy milk and bread~~
~~Mail letter~~
Make birthday cake
Call Grandma
Take dog for walk

❶ Has he cleaned the kitchen yet?

_____

❷ Has he bought milk and bread yet?

_____

❸ Has he taken the dog for a walk yet?

_____

❺ Has he mailed the letter yet?

_____

❹ Has he made the birthday cake yet?

_____

❻ Has he called his grandmother yet?

_____

47 ✓ CHECKLIST

⚙ "Yet" and "already" ☐   **Aa** Routines and chores ☐   🧩 Talking about the recent past ☐

48 Eating out

"Eating out" means having a meal outside your home, usually in a restaurant. To do this, you need to know the language for making a reservation and ordering food.

⚙ **New language** Restaurant phrases
Aa Vocabulary Food preparation
🧩 **New skill** Ordering a meal in a restaurant

48.1 KEY LANGUAGE ORDERING A MEAL

A restaurant meal often has three courses.

Have you made a reservation?

Yes, we have.

Would you like to see the menu?

Yes, please.

Are you ready to order?

Could we have a few more minutes?

For my main course, I'd like the fish. And for dessert, I'll have the apple pie.

TIP
In US English, you can use "entrée" or "main course" to describe the main dish in a meal.

How's your meal?

It's delicious, thank you.

Excuse me! Can we have the check, please?

Of course, sir.

48.2 VOCABULARY EATING OUT AND FOOD PREPARATION

appetizer (US)
starter (UK)

entrée (US)
main course (UK)

dessert

the check (US)
the bill (UK)

reservation /
booking

....

roast

bake

broil (US)
grill (UK)

boil

fry

....

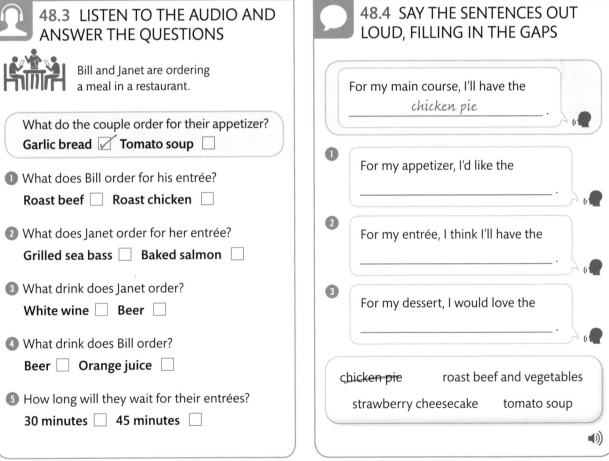

48.3 LISTEN TO THE AUDIO AND ANSWER THE QUESTIONS

Bill and Janet are ordering a meal in a restaurant.

What do the couple order for their appetizer?
Garlic bread ☑   Tomato soup ☐

1 What does Bill order for his entrée?
Roast beef ☐   Roast chicken ☐

2 What does Janet order for her entrée?
Grilled sea bass ☐   Baked salmon ☐

3 What drink does Janet order?
White wine ☐   Beer ☐

4 What drink does Bill order?
Beer ☐   Orange juice ☐

5 How long will they wait for their entrées?
30 minutes ☐   45 minutes ☐

48.4 SAY THE SENTENCES OUT LOUD, FILLING IN THE GAPS

For my main course, I'll have the
_____chicken pie_____ .

1 For my appetizer, I'd like the
_____ .

2 For my entrée, I think I'll have the
_____ .

3 For my dessert, I would love the
_____ .

chicken pie   roast beef and vegetables
strawberry cheesecake   tomato soup

48 ✓ CHECKLIST

⚙ Restaurant phrases ☐   **Aa** Food preparation ☐   🧩 Ordering a meal in a restaurant ☐

49 Achievements and ambitions

English uses different phrases to talk about future wishes or desires, definite future plans, and past achievements. Use them in conversation to talk about your life.

⚙ **New language** Desires and plans
Aa Vocabulary Travel and adventure sports
🧩 **New skill** Talking about your achievements

49.1 KEY LANGUAGE DESIRES AND PLANS

Use expressions such as "I'd like to" for desires. Use "I'm going to" for definite plans.

Have you ever worked abroad?

You want to work abroad.

No, but I'd like to work in Asia.

No, but I'm going to next year.

Your plan is to work abroad next year.

🔊

49.2 FURTHER EXAMPLES DESIRES AND PLANS

I'm very excited. We're going to hike the Inca Trail next year.

I haven't climbed Mount Fuji, but I'm going to do it this summer.

I've never been to South America, but I want to go.

I've never seen a whale. I'd like to go whale-watching later this year.

🔊

49.3 MATCH THE QUESTIONS TO THE CORRECT ANSWERS

Have you ever played golf? ⟶ No, but I'm going to watch the US Open.

No, but I love Shakespeare and I'd like to see it.

❶ Have you ever been paragliding?

No, but I want to do that next year.

❷ Have you ever seen *Hamlet*?

❸ Have you ever been to Machu Picchu?

No, but I want to go sailing in the summer.

❹ Have you ever been on a boat?

No, but we're going to go there next year.

🔊

49.4 LISTEN TO THE AUDIO AND MARK WHAT BRETT HAS OR HASN'T DONE

Radio presenter Ken Wallace
interviews stunt man Brett Ellis.

Has done ☐   Hasn't done ☐

① Has done ☐   Hasn't done ☐

② Has done ☐   Hasn't done ☐

③ Has done ☐   Hasn't done ☐

Aa 49.5 READ THE CLUES AND WRITE THE ANSWERS IN THE CORRECT PLACES ON THE GRID

Crossword grid:
1 Down/Across starting: ¹D e s ²e r t

ACROSS

① Davina is going to ride a camel across the Gobi _____ .

③ Harry wants to _____ along the Pacific Coast Highway.

⑥ Dan would like to go swimming with _____ in Mexico.

⑦ Flo would like to study _____ in Beijing.

⑨ Susie wants to see kangaroos in _____ .

DOWN

② Javier wants to speak _____ every day.

④ Ben would like to climb a _____ .

⑤ José wants to play _____ with the Dallas Cowboys.

⑧ Gary is going to _____ a short movie with his friends.

⑩ Melinda wants to _____ her boat around the world.

Word bank:
~~Desert~~   sail   dolphins   Australia   drive
football   Chinese   make   mountain   English

165

49.6 KEY LANGUAGE THINGS I'VE DONE AND WANT TO DO

Use words such as "never," "yet," or "really" to place a different emphasis on what you're saying.

I've **never** run a marathon.

"I've never ..." is stronger than "I've not ..."

I haven't seen the Pyramids of Giza **yet**.

You haven't seen the Pyramids of Giza until now, but you intend to see them one day.

I **really** want to climb Mount Everest.

Your desire to climb Mount Everest is strong.

Aa 49.7 MATCH THE PICTURES TO THE CORRECT SENTENCES

I haven't been up in a hot-air balloon, but I'm going to do that for my birthday in August.

1

I haven't traveled in a helicopter yet, but I'm going to fly over New York in one soon.

2

I haven't been to a music festival yet, but my friends really want to take me to one next summer.

3

I've never learned to ski, but my friend Sanjay is going to teach me next year.

4

I've never been on TV, but I'm going to be on a TV quiz show in a few weeks. I'm very excited.

49.8 READ THE EMAIL AND ANSWER THE QUESTIONS

John has been surfing in South Africa and Australia.
True ☐ **False** ☑

To: Jo Abernathy

Subject: Things I want to do this year

Hi Jo,

I want to plan our year, so we can do more things. We've already been surfing in Australia and Hawaii, but we haven't surfed in South Africa yet. I've also never seen a lion, so I want to go on safari. We've never done that before. Also, I know we're going to China next year, but this summer I want to go to Thailand. I'd really like to ride an elephant, and I know you haven't done that yet. What do you think?
John

1 John has never seen a lion.
True ☐ **False** ☐

2 John and Jo have been on safari before.
True ☐ **False** ☐

3 John and Jo are going to China this year.
True ☐ **False** ☐

4 John wants to go Japan this summer.
True ☐ **False** ☐

5 Jo has never been on an elephant.
True ☐ **False** ☐

49 ✓ CHECKLIST

⚙ Desires and plans ☐   **Aa** Travel and adventure sports ☐   🧩 Talking about your achievements ☐

♻ REVIEW THE ENGLISH YOU HAVE LEARNED IN UNITS 45–49

NEW LANGUAGE	SAMPLE SENTENCE	☑	UNIT
THE PRESENT PERFECT	**Tom** has just cleaned **the windows.**	☐	45.1, 45.3
THE PAST SIMPLE AND THE PRESENT PERFECT	I visited **France in 2010.** I have visited **France many times.**	☐	46.1
"YET" AND "ALREADY" WITH THE PRESENT PERFECT	**I haven't ordered the pizza** yet. **I've** already **ordered the pizza.**	☐	47.5, 47.6
ORDERING A MEAL	"Have you made a reservation?" **"Yes, I have."** **"Excuse me!** Can we have the check, please."	☐	48.1
DESIRES AND PLANS	I'd like to **work in Asia.** I'm going to **work there next year.**	☐	49.1, 49.2, 49.6

Answers

1.4
1. You **are** 40 years old.
2. I **am** from New Zealand.
3. He **is** my cousin.
4. We **are** British.
5. They **are** mechanics.
6. She **is** my sister.
7. We **are** scientists.
8. She **is** 21 years old.

1.5
1. You **are** British.
2. He **is** a farmer.
3. They **are** 13 years old.
4. We **are** French.
5. I **am** an engineer.

1.6
1. True
2. False
3. False
4. True
5. True

1.7
1. I am Jack.
2. I am 40 years old.
3. I am Canadian.
4. I am an engineer.
5. He is Jack.
6. He is 40 years old.
7. He is Canadian.
8. He is an engineer.
9. They are 40 years old.
10. They are Canadian.

1.10
Note: All answers can also be written without contractions.
1. He **isn't** playing tennis.
2. She **isn't** a waitress.
3. He **isn't** 30 years old.
4. We **aren't** teachers.
5. **I'm not** at work.
6. Lyla **isn't** a cat.

1.11
Note: All answers can also be written without contractions.
1. Kaleh isn't their mother.
2. There isn't a bank on this street.
3. That isn't his laptop.
4. They aren't her grandparents.
5. Alyssa and Logan aren't your friends.

1.14
1. Is Alvera a nurse?
2. Are those my keys?
3. Are Ruby and Farid artists?
4. Are they best friends?

1.15
1. **Is** Holly your mother?
2. **Are** they from Argentina?
3. **Are** these your dogs?
4. **Is** this Main Street?

2.4
1. He **wakes up** at 7 o'clock.
2. I **start** work at 10am.
3. They **leave** home at 8:45am.
4. We **finish** work at 4pm.
5. My friend **has** dinner at 6:30pm.
6. I **cook** dinner every night.
7. My parents **eat** lunch at 2pm.
8. Mia **gets up** at 5 o'clock.
9. My cousin **works** with animals.

2.5
1. We **leave** work at 5:30pm.
2. Pam **eats** lunch at 1:30pm.
3. We **walk** in the park.
4. His son **goes to** work at 9am.
5. My brother **leaves** work at 4:45pm.
6. They **eat** dinner at 8pm.

2.6
1. My son **watches** TV all night.
2. He **goes** shopping on Fridays.
3. We **eat** breakfast at 7am.
4. My cousin **works** inside.
5. Georgia **starts** work at 9am.
6. They **do** their chores.

2.10
1. I go to work every day.
   I do not go to work every day.
2. He watches TV in the evening.
   He doesn't watch TV in the evening.
3. They do not work in an office.
   They don't work in an office.

2.13
1. Do you like basketball?
2. Do you like running?
3. Do you like pizza?
4. Does he like basketball?
5. Does he like running?
6. Does he like pizza?
7. I don't work on the weekend.
8. I don't work on Mondays.
9. My sister doesn't work on the weekend.
10. My sister doesn't work on Mondays.
11. They don't work on the weekend.
12. They don't work on Mondays.

3.4
1. Sharon **is** reading a book.
2. I **am** carrying my laptop.
3. My cat **is** climbing a tree.
4. We **are** working at the moment.
5. They **are** having their dinner.
6. He **is** talking to his dad.
7. I **am** driving to work right now.
8. They **are** watching the film.

3.5 🔊
1. They **are coming** home now.
2. We **are playing** a board game.
3. Jamie **is cooking** dinner.
4. He **is drinking** some water.
5. We **are listening** to music.
6. I **am washing** my hair.
7. You **are winning** the game.
8. We **are visiting** New Zealand.

3.6
1. Emma
2. Max
3. Julie
4. Emma's cousin

3.10 🔊
1. We **aren't** playing with them.
2. The baby **isn't** sleeping.
3. He **isn't** watching the game.
4. You **aren't** wearing boots.
5. She **isn't** cooking lunch.
6. We **aren't** meeting right now.
7. I **am not** eating with them.

3.11 🔊
1. They **aren't going** to the park.
2. I**'m not eating** this meal.
3. You **aren't wearing** this coat again.
4. Frank's dog **isn't sitting** by the fire.
5. My dad **isn't carrying** the heavy box.

3.12
1. Dan is watching a film.
2. Manu's exercising.
3. George's playing his guitar.
4. Jamal is playing a computer game.

3.13 🔊
1. They are climbing a tree. They aren't climbing a tree.
2. They are surfing. They aren't surfing.
3. They are washing the car. They aren't washing the car.

4.5
1. Martha 2. Rachel 3. Fleur 4. Jacob

4.6 🔊
1. What are John and Mike watching? **They are watching a movie.**
2. What is Sida singing? **She is singing "Happy Birthday."**
3. Where are you going? **We are going to the store.**
4. What are Anna and Sue eating? **They are eating chocolate.**
5. What are Ali and Sam doing? **They are cooking dinner.**

4.8 🔊
1. Sam is **wearing** red pants.
2. Jack is **reading** on an e-reader.
3. You are **listening** to headphones.
4. Sam is **cleaning** her bike.
5. I am **using** my smartphone.

4.9
1. his shirt
2. a computer
3. a skirt
4. writing
5. radio
6. her laptop
7. his e-reader

4.10 🔊
1. What is Kimi cleaning?
2. What is Jill doing?
3. What is Jack using?
4. What is Max holding?
5. What is Marge carrying?

4.11 🔊
1. Emir is going to New York.
2. They are holding books.
3. She is carrying a laptop.

5.3
ACTION VERBS: **go, learn, read, eat**
STATE VERBS: **want, love, hate, remember**

5.5 🔊
1. I **have** a big house by the ocean.
2. My sister **hates** this new TV show.
3. Thomas **knows** your dad.
4. Finn **wants** a new bike.
5. I **see** the cat and dog.

5.6 🔊
1. She **is going** to the store now.
2. Fred **doesn't like** pizza.
3. I always **sing** in the bath.
4. He **is reading** a book at the moment.
5. Jo **remembers** my birthday.
6. Li **is playing** tennis at the moment.
7. We **don't want** to leave.

7.4
1. bored
2. calm
3. confident
4. stressed
5. miserable

7.5 🔊
1. Ben **is feeling** bored.
2. Luis **is feeling** irritated.
3. I **am feeling** sad.
4. You **are feeling** calm.
5. Kate and I **are feeling** happy.
6. Gina **is feeling** confident.
7. We **are feeling** excited.
8. I **am feeling** tired.

7.6

1. True
2. False
3. False
4. True
5. True
6. False
7. True
8. True

7.10 ◀))

1. Joe's **very** unhappy.
2. Bella and Edith are **really** sad.
3. Lin is **very** nervous.
4. She is **very** confident.
5. They're **so** tired.

7.11 ◀))

1. I'm at the airport. I'm waiting for the flight. I don't have a book. There's nothing to do. I'm really **bored**.
2. I'm watching a movie on TV. It's a love story. The man and his wife are in different countries. They're very **sad**.
3. We're at the concert. We're waiting for my favorite band in the world to come on stage. We're at the front. I'm so **excited**.
4. I'm at the supermarket. There's no milk, no butter, no flour, and no sugar. All the things that I need for the cake. I'm so **angry**.
5. I'm waiting to meet my new boss. She's talking to everyone in the office. I don't know what to say to her. I'm very **nervous**.

09

9.4 ◀))

1. Sarah and I normally **play** tennis on Wednesdays, but today we **are swimming**.
2. Today, I **am having** soup for lunch, but I usually **have** a sandwich.

3. We often **watch** TV in the evenings, but tonight we **are having** a party.
4. Ben and Tom usually **work** until 6pm, but tonight they **are working** until 9pm.
5. Melanie **is skiing** in France this winter, but she normally **goes** to Italy.
6. Today, you **are drinking** water, but you often **have** coffee after lunch.

9.6

1. Denzel **is seeing a show.**
2. Selma **is doing her project.**
3. Marlow **is playing hockey.**
4. Roxy **is making dinner.**
5. Rainey **is eating with friends.**
6. Malala is **having coffee**.
7. Altan is **taking a break.**

9.7

1. A 2. B 3. C

9.8 ◀))

1. Sally usually **swims**, but right now **she's playing** soccer.
2. Abe normally **reads**, but tonight **he's listening** to music.
3. They often **play** golf, but today **they're playing** hockey.
4. I usually **take** a shower, but today **I'm taking** a bath.

11

11.2 ◀))

1. My brother isn't **feeling** very well this morning.
2. George **is** sick, so he's staying in bed today.
3. I **am** sick, so I'm not going to work.
4. Ayshah **isn't** feeling well, so she's going home.
5. Luca and Ben **aren't** feeling well today.

11.5 ◀))

1. Mary's back **hurts**.
2. John has a **broken** leg.
3. I've got a **pain** in my finger.
4. She has a terrible **toothache**.

11.6 ◀))

1. I have a pain in my arm.
2. John has got an earache.
3. His head hurts.
4. Aziz has got a pain in his back.

13

13.3 ◀))

1. The weather is beautiful here. It's hot and sunny, and we're having a great time.
2. There's a lot of snow, so the children are having a great time. They want to learn how to ski.
3. This is a beautiful place, but I really want it to be sunny. It's dark and cloudy all the time.

13.4 ◀))

1. Oh no! I hate this weather. It's **raining** again.
2. I can't ride my bike in these conditions. It's too **foggy**.
3. Be careful! There's **ice** on the road.
4. Wow! It's really **stormy** outside today.

13.6

1. freezing
2. cold
3. hot
4. boiling
5. warm

13.7

1. 55°F
2. Seattle
3. Anchorage
4. Houston

13.8 🔊
1 There's a lot of ice.
2 It's very windy.
3 It's very rainy.
4 It's sunny.
5 There are a lot of clouds.

15

15.4 🔊
1 An **elephant** is larger than a **lion**.
2 **Three** o'clock is earlier than **seven** o'clock.
3 **Ice cream** is colder than **coffee**.
4 A **mouse** is smaller than a **cat**.

15.5
1 thinner 2 lower 3 higher
4 larger 5 later 6 easier
7 earlier 8 hotter 9 closer

15.9 🔊
1 The Hotel Supreme is very expensive. It's **more expensive than** the Motel Excelsior.
2 The physics exam is really difficult. It's **more difficult than** the biology exam.
3 Your dress is very beautiful. It's **more beautiful than** my dress.
4 This TV program is really interesting. It's **more interesting than** the other ones.

15.10 🔊
1 This laptop is **more expensive than** this phone.
2 Seven o'clock is **later than** three o'clock.
3 A game of chess is **more difficult than** a game of cards.
4 A horse is **bigger than** a rabbit.

15.11
1 False 2 True 3 False 4 False

15.12 🔊
1 Paris is **more beautiful** than Dallas.
2 Noon is **earlier** than 5pm.
3 A cheetah is **faster** than a bear.
4 Gold is **more expensive** than silver.
5 Rock is **harder** than paper.
6 Water is **warmer** than ice.
7 Skiing is **more exciting** than walking.

16

16.5
1 Ben
2 Sarah
3 Joel
4 Ben
5 Sarah

16.6 🔊
1 The African elephant is the **heaviest** animal on land.
2 The **fastest** animal in the world is the peregrine falcon.
3 The **longest** word in the English dictionary has 45 letters.
4 The Sahara is the **biggest** desert in the world.
5 The giraffe is the **tallest** animal on Earth.

16.10 🔊
1 Antarctica is **the coldest place on Earth.**
2 Mumbai is **the biggest city in India.**
3 Alaska is **the largest state in the US.**
4 The inland taipan is **the most dangerous snake in the world.**

16.11
1 The Grand
2 The Plaza
3 The Plaza
4 The Grand
5 The Rialto

16.12 🔊
1 Istanbul is a very large city. It is **the largest** city in Europe.
2 The Missouri River is 2,540 miles long. It is **the longest** river in North America.
3 The cheetah is a very fast animal. It is **the fastest** land animal on Earth.
4 The Kali Gandaki Gorge is 3.46 miles deep. It is **the deepest** gorge in the world.

18

18.3 🔊
1 Do you want to visit New York **and** Chicago?
2 Would you like to study chemistry **or** physics?
3 Would you like a burger **and** a soda?
4 Do you want to go home **or** go to a restaurant?

18.6 🔊
1 **What** is the biggest country in Africa?
2 **What** would you like to eat for your dinner?
3 **Which** jacket do you want to wear, the blue one or the red one?
4 **Which** is you favorite color, red, green, yellow, or blue?

18.9
1 John's Bar has the best music.
2 The Big Cahuna is the farthest from the beach.
3 The Seaview Café has the best ice cream.
4 The Big Cahuna has the worst food.
5 The Little Olive has the best seafood.

18.10
1 Taipei
2 Suriname
3 Sahara
4 Eiffel Tower
5 K2

19

19.3
1. 4,500
2. 467,000
3. 989
4. 72,427
5. 4,125,025

19.4 🔊
1. Three thousand, one hundred and seven.
2. Twenty-three thousand, four hundred and seventeen.
3. Three hundred and forty-five thousand, nine hundred and seventy-two.
4. Twenty-three million, four hundred and fifty-six thousand, nine hundred and eighty-seven.

21

21.3
1. B
2. F
3. A
4. G
5. E
6. C
7. D

21.6
1. 1976
2. 1993
3. 1996
4. 2004
5. 2008

21.7 🔊
1. My birthday is on December 5.
2. My birthday is on the 11th of March.

3. My meeting is on December 5.
4. My meeting is on the 11th of March.
5. Nami's birthday is on December 5.
6. Nami's birthday is on the 11th of March.
7. Nami's meeting is on December 5.
8. Nami's meeting is on the 11th of March.
9. I was born 20 years ago.
10. I was born 41 years ago.
11. He was born 20 years ago.
12. He was born 41 years ago.

22

22.4 🔊
1. You **were** at the museum last week.
2. There **were** five people here yesterday.
3. The students **were** there on Monday morning.
4. My mom **was** an artist in the 1990s.
5. I **was** in college in 1989.
6. Sal and I **were** at the theater last night.
7. My dad **was** a builder until 1995.

22.5
1. True
2. False
3. False
4. False

22.6
1. 1918
2. 1964
3. 1969
4. 1994

22.10 🔊
1. They **weren't** very good at science.
2. I **wasn't** in Canada in 2002.
3. You **weren't** at the party last night.
4. We **weren't** in our house last year.
5. There **wasn't** a restaurant near the river.

22.11 🔊
1. Was he a good builder?
2. Were they late this morning?
3. Was she at a meeting yesterday?
4. Were you happy in college?
5. Were we in New Zealand for two weeks?
6. Were you in the swimming pool?

22.12
1. B
2. B
3. A
4. A

22.13 🔊
1. I was a student last year.
2. I was a student in 2008.
3. I was a student for four years.
4. They were students last year.
5. They were students in 2008.
6. They were students for four years.
7. I was in Australia last year.
8. I was in Australia in 2008.
9. I was in Australia for four years.
10. They were in Australia last year.
11. They were in Australia in 2008.
12. They were in Australia for four years.
13. They were good friends last year.
14. They were good friends in 2008.
15. They were good friends for four years.

23

23.4 🔊
1. The music was good, but I **didn't dance** very much.
2. My friend **didn't listen** to the band on Saturday night.
3. Last week, I **cleaned** my brother's new car for him.
4. Did you **watch** a fun movie last night?
5. Ben and Franklin **played** tennis for five hours yesterday.

23.7 🔊
① On Tuesday morning, she **played** squash.
② On Tuesday afternoon, she **phoned** her boss.
③ On Wednesday, she **tried** sushi at a Japanese restaurant.
④ On Thursday morning, she **cleaned** the bathroom.
⑤ On Thursday night, she **visited** Aziz in hospital.
⑥ On Friday, she **invited** friends to her birthday party.
⑦ On Saturday, she **walked** in the park.
⑧ On Sunday, she **cooked** dinner for her parents.

23.8
① 1974
② 1989
③ 1991
④ 1975
⑤ 1993
⑥ 1995

23.10 🔊
① She moved to the US when she was 19 years old.
② They started swimming when they were 25 years old.
③ We visited Japan when we were 27 years old.
④ I received this gift when I was 31 years old.

23.11 🔊
① She moved to New York in 1996.
② She visited Asia in 2008.
③ She started her first job in 2010.

24

24.4 🔊
① I could cook Italian food.
② We couldn't play the piano.
③ She could paint a picture.
④ They couldn't make a cake.

24.5
① do mathematics
② ride a horse
③ three languages

24.6 🔊
1. When I was five, I couldn't play chess.
2. When I was five, I couldn't ride a bike.
3. When I was five, I couldn't swim.
4. When I was five, I couldn't skate.
5. When I was seven, I couldn't play chess.
6. When I was seven, I couldn't ride a bike.
7. When I was seven, I couldn't swim.
8. When I was seven, I couldn't skate.
9. When you were five, you could play chess.
10. When you were five, you could ride a bike.
11. When you were five, you could swim.
12. When you were five, you could skate.
13. When you were seven, you could play chess.
14. When you were seven, you could ride a bike.
15. When you were seven, you could swim.
16. When you were seven, you could skate.

26

26.4 🔊
① begin
② break
③ take
④ sell
⑤ buy
⑥ get
⑦ write
⑧ make
⑨ sit

26.5
① C
② G
③ B
④ A
⑤ F
⑥ E
⑦ D

26.6
Wow! This morning a bear **ate** my breakfast. We are in the Redwood Park and last night we camped in the forest. We **made** a fire and it was very quiet, so my friend and I **slept** well. Later on, we **went** to the river to get water. When we got back to the tent, we **saw** the bear. I **felt** really scared. We **ran** back to the campsite and we are safe now!

26.9 🔊
① **First** Sheila put her best clothes on.
② **First** do your homework. **Then** go out and play.
③ Ben passed his test. **Next** he bought a car.
④ Eat dinner. **After that** you can have some dessert.
⑤ **First** he ate a large breakfast.

26.10 🔊
① **After that** they got lost. Then they decided to camp and put the tent up.
② They were scared of the sounds in the forest. But **finally** they went to sleep.
③ **In the morning** they washed in the river. They went back to their tent for food.
④ **After that** they saw a bear eating their food. After that it walked into the forest.
⑤ **Finally** Harold and Jack arrived safely back at the campsite.

26.13 🔊
① What did she eat? **She ate a burger and fries.**

2 How much did he spend? **He spent about $500.**

3 What time did you leave the bar? **I left around 11pm.**

4 Did they go by bus? **Yes, because there were no trains.**

5 Did I get any mail? **You got three letters.**

6 Did we win the competition? **No, we lost.**

26.14 ◀))

1 When **did the movie begin?**

2 Which **shirt did he choose?**

3 What **did she eat last night?**

4 What **did she read this morning?**

5 How many **fish did Aia catch at the lake?**

6 Who **did you see at the party last night?**

7 What **did he give his brother?**

26.15

1 a red dress

2 a watch

3 Sam

4 pizza

5 jazz

28

28.3

1 C

2 B

3 D

4 E

5 A

28.5

1 False

2 True

3 True

4 True

5 True

6 False

28.6 ◀))

1. The movie is about three characters.
2. The movie is about a court case.
3. The movie is about a love story.
4. The play is about three characters.
5. The play is about a court case.
6. The play is about a love story.
7. It's a movie about three characters.
8. It's a movie about a court case.
9. It's a movie about a love story.
10. It's a play about three characters.
11. It's a play about a court case.
12. It's a play about a love story.

28.7

1 Millie enjoys singing.

2 Millie learns to sing in her bedroom.

3 The name of her music teacher is Miss Cafferty.

4 The villain is Miss Cafferty.

5 No. Millie is played by a child.

28.8 ◀))

1 Millie **hates** singing.

2 Millie has **ugly** costumes.

3 Many of the actors were **terrible**.

4 The songs are very **bad**.

5 I really **hated** the music.

28.9

1 villain

2 documentary

3 comedy

4 play

5 author

6 adventure

29

29.4

1 B

2 A

3 D

4 C

5 E

29.5 ◀))

1 Did I have lunch today? **No, you didn't.**

2 Did the dog eat its dinner? **Yes, it did.**

3 Did they go to Venezuela? **No, they didn't.**

4 Did we win the competition? **Yes, we did.**

29.6 ◀))

1 Did they give Ellie a present?

2 Did you stay in an expensive hotel?

3 Did his mother buy lots of postcards?

4 Did your brother climb a mountain?

5 Did their parents take lots of photos?

29.9 ◀))

1 How did you get to the station? **By taxi.**

2 Where did you stay? **In the Hotel Bella Vista.**

3 Why did you stay there? **Because it was cheap.**

4 Who did you go on vacation with? **Daniella and Toni.**

29.10

1 By boat

2 On Saturday

3 Macy's

4 Some clothes

5 Oysters

29.11 ◀))

1 Who **did you go on vacation with**?

2 Where **did you stay in London**?

3 What **did you eat in Chinatown**?

4 How **long did you go abroad** for?

5 When **did you leave the US**?

30

30.2

1 True

2 False

3 True
4 False
5 False

30.4 ◀))
1 My **qualifications** include degrees in biology and chemistry.
2 The interview at the bank went really well. I've **got the job**.
3 The manager read my **résumé** and said it was really good.
4 I can **start** the job in January.
5 You need to **have an interview** before you can get the job.

30.5
1 C
2 B
3 E
4 F
5 A
6 D

31

31.5
1 False
2 True
3 True
4 False
5 True

31.6 ◀))
1 What **did Sharon get yesterday?**
2 What **did your boss have this morning?**
3 What **do you want?**
4 Who **did the staff phone last month?**
5 Who **did you see on TV last night?**

31.10 ◀))
1 What did the manager say?
2 Which customer did you speak to?

3 Who gave Emma that book?
4 What started at 7am?

31.11 ◀))
1 What did the dog break?
2 Who ate the last piece of cake?
3 Which TV program starts at 9pm?
4 What did they eat?
5 Who has a better job now?
6 Who did you speak to yesterday?

31.12 ◀))
1 What **did Arjun start last month?**
2 What **does the office have?**
3 Who **is waiting outside?**
4 What **does Mark want to be?**
5 What **does the boss want this year?**

32

32.3 ◀))
1 Please ask **someone** to phone Mr. Richards right away.
2 Mrs. Turner didn't give **anyone** any work to do this week.
3 Can I give **anyone** a lift to the station tomorrow morning?
4 Mr. Phillips needs **someone** to go with him to the hospital.
5 I'm sorry, but there isn't **anyone** in the office at the moment.

32.5
1 **Somebody** in room 212 needs a new computer.
2 Theodore tells **someone** the good news about the business.
3 **Everyone** is going for lunch at the restaurant to celebrate Daniella's birthday.
4 **Nobody** closed the window last night before they left the office.
5 **Everyone** knows that we have a new office.

32.6 ◀))
1. Everybody went to the meeting.
2. Everybody went to the party.
3. Everybody wrote to the customer.
4. Everybody finished their work today.
5. Someone went to the meeting.
6. Someone went to the party.
7. Someone wrote to the customer.
8. Someone finished their work today.
9. Nobody went to the meeting.
10. Nobody went to the party.
11. Nobody wrote to the customer.
12. Nobody finished their work today.

33

33.4 ◀))
1 I was very tired last night. **Were you?**
2 We didn't go to the party. **Didn't you?**
3 Frank wasn't feeling well. **He wasn't?**
4 That cat likes its new food. **Does it?**

33.5 ◀))
1 **Was** it?
2 There **is**?
3 **Did** you?

35

35.4 ◀))
1 John's cousins **are coming** to the party tomorrow.
2 **I am going** to the dentist tomorrow morning.
3 My family and I **are visiting** my grandma on Saturday.
4 The managers in my office **are having** a meeting this afternoon.
5 A famous band **is playing** in Central Park this weekend.
6 He **is studying** for his test tomorrow.

35.5

Ⓐ 3
Ⓑ 6
Ⓒ 1
Ⓓ 4
Ⓔ 7
Ⓕ 2
Ⓖ 5

35.8 ◀))

① Sorry, I can't. I'm visiting my parents this evening.
② I'd like to, but I'm going to France this weekend.
③ That sounds nice, but I'm going swimming on Tuesday.
④ I'd love to, but I'm looking after my nephew tomorrow.

35.9 ◀))

① I'd like to, but **I'm going to dinner with Marco and Olivia**.
② Sorry, I can't. **I'm going to lunch with Aziz**.
③ That would be fun, but **I'm going to the theater to see a musica**l.
④ That sounds nice, but **I'm looking after Sandy's baby**.
⑤ I'd like to, but **I'm going to a yoga class**.

36

36.4 ◀))

① I **am not going** to eat sushi for dinner.
② Debra **is going to get** a new job soon.
③ My friends **are going to cook** a meal for me next week.
④ Manuel **is going to learn** how to scuba dive this summer.
⑤ We **are going to travel** to Dubai in December.

36.5

① False
② True
③ True
④ False
⑤ False

36.8

① He is going to paint his bedroom by the end of this month.
② He is going to join a gym by this time next month.
③ He is going to book a vacation by the end of March.
④ He is going to get fit by the summer.
⑤ He is going to buy a new car by December.

36.9 ◀))

① Tim is going to buy a new boat by October.
② Sally and Jane are going to go on vacation on the weekend.
③ I am going to write a book by this time next year.
④ We are going to run a marathon tomorrow.

36.10

① Jack is going to join a gym before the summer.
② Samantha is going to write music at weekends.
③ Debbie is going to travel more in the winter.
④ Joseph is going to learn how to cook by this time next month.

37

37.3 ◀))

① Watch out! You **are going to step into** that puddle.
② The dog **isn't going to eat** its food. I think it's sick.

③ Oh no! She **is going to fall off** the ladder.
④ John is terrible at golf! He **isn't going to win** the tournament.
⑤ It's very windy! His umbrella is **going to blow away**.
⑥ You're carrying too much. You **are going to drop** everything.

37.4 ◀))

① John and Jill are putting their coats on. They **are** going to leave now.
② I saw the weather forecast. It **is** going to snow this afternoon.
③ It's my birthday, so I **am** going to get a present from my husband.
④ Larry and John have gone home to get their tennis rackets. They **are** going to play tennis.

37.5

① He is **not going to** be in the next Olympics.
② Marco **is going to** study art at university.
③ He **is not going to** be the main character in a musical.
④ Marco **is going to** fail his English exam.
⑤ He **is going to** play soccer next weekend.

37.6

① fall over
② crash into
③ fail
④ pass
⑤ break

37.7 ◀))

① The man is going to **fall into** the pond.
② The snowman is going to **fall over**.
③ It is going to **rain** later today.
④ The boy in the blue shirt is going to **win**.
⑤ The store is going to **close** now.

37.8 🔊
1. I am going to be late for work.
2. I am going to make a fruit cake.
3. I am going to play soccer.
4. Sheila is going to be late for work.
5. Sheila is going to make a fruit cake.
6. Sheila is going to play soccer.
7. We are going to be late for work.
8. We are going to make a fruit cake.
9. We are going to play soccer.
10. They are going to be late for work.
11. They are going to make a fruit cake.
12. They are going to play soccer.

39

39.4 🔊
1 John **will not eat** pizza.
2 Maria **will enjoy** the new dance class.
3 Susie and Bella **will be** early for work this week.
4 The children **will not understand** this information.

39.5
1 He'll bring chocolates.
2 She'll make a salad.
3 He'll not bring anything.
4 I'll bring drinks.
5 They'll buy some cheese.

39.6
1 Who will find the party music?
Marsha will do it.
2 Who will bring the party games? **Sam will do it.**
3 Who will bake a birthday cake?
Jenny's mother will do it.
4 Who will cook the food? **Jenny's brother will do it.**

39.10 🔊
1 Diane works very hard. **I think she'll pass her exams.**

2 Chiara loves traveling. **I think she'll enjoy visiting Rome.**
3 Carl failed his driver's test again. **I don't think he'll ever pass it.**
4 Georgia can't sing very well. **I don't think she'll be in the musical.**

39.12 🔊
1 Bob is going to **eat** all his dinner.
2 It is going to **snow** this afternoon.
3 The dog will **eat** these leftovers.
4 The car is going to **turn** left.
5 John thinks he will **go out** tonight.

40

40.4 🔊
1 It's my birthday, **so I'll cut the cake.**
2 I forgot my swimming trunks, **so I won't go in the water.**
3 I don't have any money, **so I won't go shopping.**
4 I can't find my train ticket, **so I'll get the bus.**

40.5
1 C 2 E 3 D 4 A 5 B

40.6 🔊
1 In that case we'll **go** by bus.
2 In that case I'll **have** tea.
3 In that case we'll **eat** at home.
4 In that case I'll **listen to** music.

40.9
1 False
2 True
3 False
4 True
5 True
6 True

40.10 🔊
1 I think I'll **have milk**.
2 I think I'll **leave at 6:30pm**.

3 I think I'll **play with Cassie**.
4 I think I'll watch **the news**.
5 I think I'll **go home**.

41

41.4 🔊
1 My dad might give me some money.
2 Helen might pass her driving test.
3 I might not eat a chocolate bar.
4 They might not have a party.

41.5
1 we will
2 I'll bring
3 I won't
4 We might

41.6
1 They won't make dinner.
  They might make dinner.
2 He won't be late again.
  He will be late again.
3 You might remember that.
  You will remember that.
4 She won't become a teacher.
  She will become a teacher.
5 We won't win the game.
  We might win the game.
6 The dog might eat this food.
  The dog will eat this food.

41.8 🔊
1 Where will you live next year? **I don't know. I might live in Boston.**
2 What will you do before you start college? **I might get a summer job. I'm not sure.**
3 How much money are you taking on vacation? **I'm not sure. I might take about $300.**

41.9
1 She might.
2 No, they're not.
3 He might.
4 No, she won't.
5 No, she won't.

41.10 ◀))
1 Aban might learn French.
2 Aban won't run a marathon.
3 Nadiya will become a doctor.
4 Nadiya might write a book.
5 Nadiya won't do a bungee jump.
6 Jack will get a dog.
7 Jack might buy a motorcycle.
8 Jack won't move house.

42

42.4 ◀))
1 You shouldn't open this door.
2 She should play the guitar every day.
3 He shouldn't wear that tie with that shirt.
4 You should take a tablet twice a day.
5 They shouldn't ride their bikes here.

42.5 ◀))
1 We **shouldn't** swim at this beach.
2 People **should** be quiet in the library.
3 Shoppers **should** email.
4 They **should not** walk on the ice.
5 You **shouldn't** drive too fast.

42.6 ◀))
1 I've got too many clothes. **You should sell some of them.**
2 I eat too much junk food. **You should eat more fruit.**
3 I don't know my neighbors. **You should have a block party.**
4 I feel tired all the time. **You should get more sleep.**
5 I need more exercise. **You should join a gym.**

6 I'm so lonely. **You should get a dog.**
7 I've nothing to wear tonight. **You should go shopping.**

42.7
1 pay $10
2 finish his work
3 get up earlier
4 use a friend's computer
5 speak clearly

42.8 ◀))
1 People **should** visit the library more often.
2 People **should** have a shower before swimming.
3 You **shouldn't** eat anything in a laboratory.
4 You **shouldn't** go through that blue door.
5 Students **shouldn't** speak during their exams.

43

43.4 ◀))
1 I didn't pass my driving test last week. **Oh well, you could take it again next month.**
2 I haven't got any nice clothes. **You could buy some new ones.**
3 I can never remember people's names. **You could write them down after you meet them.**
4 I never know what time it is. **You could buy a watch.**
5 Oh no. I forgot to lock the front door. **We could go back to your house now.**

43.5 ◀))
1 You could **save $10 a week.**
2 You could **take him with you.**
3 You could **eat it inside.**
4 You could **share with a friend.**
5 You could **write 500 words every day.**

43.8 ◀))
1 You don't know what to do for the summer. You could **get a job** or **travel.**
2 What are you going to make for dinner tonight? You could cook **chicken** or **beef.**
3 You want to be a better tennis player. You could **have some lessons** or **play more often.**
4 You can't wake up in the mornings. You could **set an alarm** or **go to bed earlier.**

43.9
1 get his children to help; get a cleaner
2 look in the newspaper; look at a website
3 read more English books; email a friend
4 take the stairs; walk to the store

45

45.5 ◀))
1 We **have not mopped** the floor.
2 Tim **has left** the door open.
3 You **have changed** the sheets.
4 Sheila **has eaten** her dinner.
5 Dad **has not painted** the fence.
6 I **have vacuumed** the living room.
7 Aziz **has watered** the plants.

45.6
1 They haven't cleaned the car.
   Have they cleaned the car?
2 You have mopped the floor.
   You haven't mopped the floor.
3 I have taken the garbage out.
   Have you taken the garbage out?
4 You haven't painted the house.
   Have you painted the house?
5 John has cooked the dinner.
   John hasn't cooked the dinner.

45.7
1 gone
2 had
3 closed
4 eaten
5 been
6 kept
7 seen
8 done

45.8 ◀))
1 We have **cooked** dinner for you.
2 Ben and Ellen **have** gone to the supermarket.
3 The children have **seen** the movie.
4 Sheila has **cleaned** the bathroom.
5 The dog **hasn't** eaten all its food.
6 They've **been** to the mall to buy you a present.

45.9
1 No, they haven't.
2 No, she hasn't.
3 Yes, he has.
4 Yes, she has.
5 No, he hasn't.

45.10 ◀))
1 cleaned
2 washed
3 cooked
4 changed
5 mopped
6 walked
7 cleared
8 brushed

45.11 ◀))
1 The children have **cleaned** the car.
2 The cat has **eaten** all its food.
3 Jemma has **broken** the window.
4 Jill has **tidied** her desk.
5 Paul has **left** his wallet on top of the car.

46

46.4 ◀))
1 I love the movie *Casablanca*. I **have watched** it more than nine times.
2 Our dog Rex **ate** all Mary's birthday cake last night.
3 Jack **didn't visit** the Colosseum when we were in Rome last year. He was too sick.
4 **Did you go** to the swimming pool downtown yesterday?

46.5 ◀))
1 Yes, she has been **bungee jumping** many times.
2 Yes, **he visited Yosemite National Park** in 2014.
3 Yes, **I saw** *Gone with the Wind* last night.
4 No, **I have not been paragliding**.
5 Yes, Mia **has been scuba diving** many times.

46.8 ◀))
1 Manuela and Giorgio have **gone** to the movies. They're meeting you there.
2 There's lots of food in the fridge because Ayida's **been** to the supermarket.
3 I've **been** to the library. Look at all the books I have!
4 Mary and Joe have **gone** to a nightclub. They'll be back after midnight.

46.9
1 We haven't been
2 We've eaten
3 We visited
4 We went

46.10
1 False
2 True
3 True
4 True

46.11 ◀))
1 She hasn't **been** to the circus.
2 I **met** my best friend when I was six.
3 You **ate** all the chocolate last night.
4 He hasn't **tried** paragliding.

47

47.3 ◀))
1 Alvita is very happy. She **won** the prize for the best chocolate cake yesterday.
2 This is a great party. I **have met** lots of really fun and interesting people.
3 Martha looks happy. She **has been** to the movies with Miles.
4 Mary can't drive. She **fell** and **broke** her arm last week.

47.4 ◀))
1 She hasn't played in any competitions.
2 She broke her leg.
3 She didn't play tennis for three months.
4 She has missed two grand slams.
5 She went to the Caribbean.

47.8 ◀))
1 Am I too late to play football? **No, the game hasn't started yet.**
2 Has Amy learned how to drive yet? **No, not yet.**
3 Can you send an email to Rachel? **I've already done it.**
4 Have you watched this movie? **Yes, I've already seen it.**

47.9
1 True
2 False
3 False
4 True
5 False

47.10

1. He has already cleaned the kitchen.
2. He has already bought milk and bread.
3. He hasn't taken the dog for a walk yet.
4. He hasn't made the birthday cake yet.
5. He has already mailed the letter.
6. He hasn't phoned his grandma yet.

48

48.3

1. Roast beef
2. Baked salmon
3. White wine
4. Orange juice
5. 30 minutes

48.4 ◀))

1. For my appetizer, I'd like the **tomato soup**.
2. For my entrée, I think I'll have the **roast beef and vegetables**.
3. For my dessert, I would love the **strawberry cheesecake**.

49

49.3 ◀))

1. Have you ever been paragliding? **No, but I want to do that next year.**
2. Have you ever seen *Hamlet*? **No, but I love Shakespeare and I'd like to see it.**
3. Have you ever been to Machu Picchu? **No, but we're going to go there next year.**
4. Have you ever been on a boat? **No, but I want to go sailing in the summer.**

49.4

1. Hasn't done
2. Has done
3. Hasn't done

49.5

1. Desert
2. English
3. drive
4. mountain
5. football
6. dolphins
7. Chinese
8. make
9. Australia
10. sail

49.7 ◀))

1. I've never learned to ski, but my friend Sanjay is going to teach me next year.
2. I haven't been up in a hot-air balloon, but I'm going to do that for my birthday in August.
3. I've never been on TV, but I'm going to be on a TV quiz show in a few weeks. I'm very excited.
4. I haven't been to a music festival yet, but my friends really want to take me to one next summer.

49.8

1. True
2. False
3. False
4. False
5. True

Index

All entries are indexed by unit number. Main entries are highlighted in **bold**.

Acknowledgments

The publisher would like to thank:
Jo Kent, Trish Burrow, and Emma Watkins for additional text; Thomas Booth, Helen Fanthorpe, Helen Leech, Carrie Lewis, and Vicky Richards for editorial assistance; Stephen Bere, Sarah Hilder, Amy Child, Fiona Macdonald, and Simon Murrell for additional design work; Simon Mumford for maps and national flags; Peter Chrisp for fact checking; Penny Hands, Amanda Learmonth, and Carrie Lewis for proofreading; Elizabeth Wise for indexing; Tatiana Boyko, Rory Farrell, Clare Joyce, and Viola Wang for additional illustrations; Liz Hammond for editing audio scripts and managing audio recordings; Hannah Bowen and Scarlett O'Hara for compiling audio scripts; Heather Hughes, Tommy Callan, Tom Morse, Gillian Reid, and Sonia Charbonnier for creative technical support; Shipra Jain, Roohi Rais, Anita Yadav, Manish Upreti, Nehal Verma, Jaileen Kaur, Tushar Kansal, Vishal Bhatia, Nisha Shaw, and Ankita Yada for technical assistance.